BEYOND THE CODE

Using Sacred Geometric Designs
-to access, Art, Language, Music, and Movement
-to access other Dimension, Universes, and Source

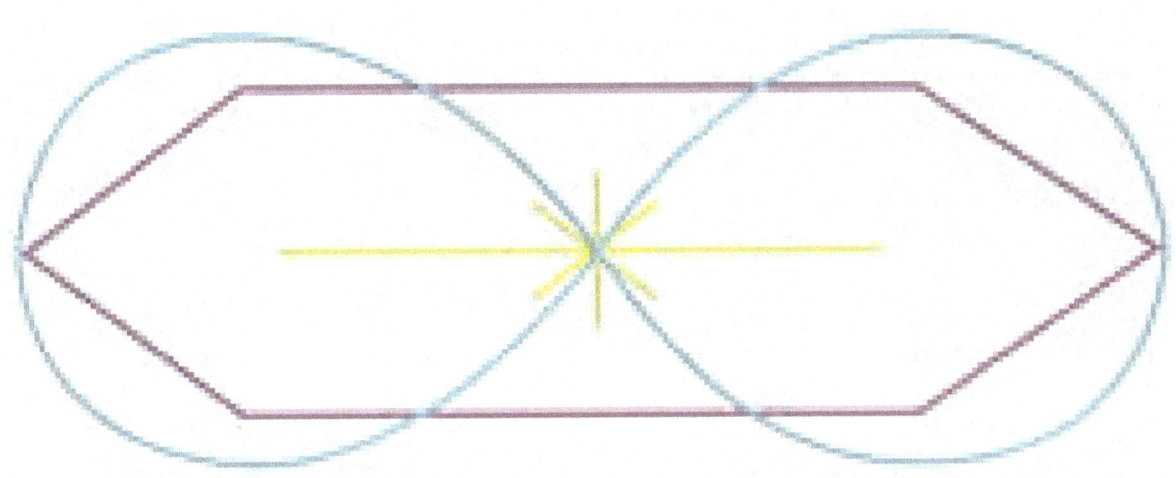

DONNA LINN

Beyond the Code

This book is written to provide information and motivation to readers. Its purpose is not to render any type of psychological, legal, or professional advice of any kind. The content is the sole opinion and expression of the author, and not necessarily that of the publisher.

Copyright © 2025 by Donna Linn.

All rights reserved. No part of this book may be reproduced, transmitted, or distributed in any form by any means, including, but not limited to, recording, photocopying, or taking screenshots of parts of the book, without prior written permission from the author or the publisher. Brief quotations for noncommercial purposes, such as book reviews, permitted by Fair Use of the U.S. Copyright Law, are allowed without written permissions, as long as such quotations do not cause damage to the book's commercial value. For permissions, write to the publisher, whose address is stated below.

Printed in the United States of America.

ISBN 978-1-64552-264-5 (Paperback)
ISBN 978-1-64552-263-8 (Digital)

Lettra Press books may be ordered through booksellers or by contacting:

Lettra Press LLC
30 N Gould St. Suite 4753
Sheridan, WY 82801
1 307-200-3414 | info@lettrapress.com
www.lettrapress.com

TABLE OF CONTENTS

Acknowledgments
Forward
Preface

PART ONE

Introduction
Explanation
Discussion

PART TWO

A1-Z4
AA-1—II-4

PART THREE

Portals, Gateways, Transits, Accelerators, Links, Stand-Alones

PART FOUR

PRL1-GW-3
AC-1-ST-2

PART FIVE

Epilogue
Bibliography
About the Author

Reprinted with Permission for noncommercial personal use only. From the Book: Beyond the Code © 2012 Donna Linn

Reprinted with Permission for noncommercial personal use only. From the Book: Beyond the Code © 2012 Donna Linn

ABOUT BEYOND THE CODE

To some, lines and shapes make geometric designs. Channeling her guides, Donna has brought forth sacred artwork that raises vibration, balances energy, opens gateways and portals, and heals on a multidimensional level. Connecting with these symbols creates a vibration that I have not experienced before.—Matthew Pierce, IT consultant

The images in the book are mesmerizing. The depth is astounding. They make you feel like you can fall into them and discover another world that you never know existed—the world inside yourself.—Arthur Graye, Artist-Green Man Studio, spiritual healer and reader.

This book is a sacred geometry masterpiece. I can feel the energy in the images and love working with them. I remember the day we held a healing arts fair at my Center. The holistic practitioners were playing with these images and sharing their experiences. They were sharing how they could feel the power and healing energy coming from the images. It was an extraordinary day at the Center. This is a book you must have if you are a Holistic Practitioner or interested in working with higher vibration energy and want to become aware of other dimensions.--Joy Kauf, owner, Miracles of Joy metaphysical store and Spiritual Center

These dynamic and engaging pictures reflect a knowing and inner balance that the author captures through her brilliant use of colors and shapes. I highly recommend this book for all those who wish to achieve a higher state of consciousness by color stimulation.—Mary Fritze, D. C.

The diagrams in Donna's book are devices that will transport you to other places, inner realms, and new states of consciousness. The gateways within them are simply amazing: if you have any sense of adventure whatsoever, I highly recommend working with this book!—Tia Adams, spiritual healer

Reprinted with Permission for noncommercial personal use only. From the Book: Beyond the Code © 2012 Donna Linn

ACKNOWLEDGEMENTS

"Miracles of Joy" metaphysical store and Spiritual Center, and Joy—for facilitating interesting classes, for space to grow, and for being a "home away from home"

CeAnn/Malachite—for prodding me to stretch myself and for giving me "hints" about this book.

Matthew—for introducing me to ways to play with these drawings

Shannon—for consistently giving me feedback on the drawings, for helping me put the drawings in place in this book

Angie—for her wonderful presence and feedback on these drawings.

"The Thursdays"—for friendship, and being willing to play with the drawings and tell me what they felt about them

Christina—for believing in me and my projects, sight unseen

Chelsea—who took my less than perfect drawings and made them into perfect representations.

Deborah—for asking good questions

Susan—as always, a friend

To the unseen Beings who "teased" me into being so interested, I took up the challenge—and then found out what I had done

To everyone else who looked at my drawings—and were interested and supportive

Reprinted with Permission for noncommercial personal use only. From the Book: Beyond the Code © 2012 Donna Linn

FORWARD

We first met Donna when she showed up at one of the channeling classes at "Miracles of Joy" that would later be lovingly called "The Thursdays". This quiet little lady would show up and in the entire two-hour meeting, we were lucky to get "My name is Donna" out of her. None of us in that class, including Donna, had any idea what energy and information she would bring through.

We would sit and stare at these drawings, and give her feedback as to what we were feeling with each one. She brought in a light board and colored sheets to put behind the acetate drawings to see if color affected the feel. She would place the drawings in the center of the room, and with ninja-like stealth, switch colors and crystals in and out of them to play with how that would feel.

What did we experience? Some would be pulled into the drawings, some would feel massive amounts of energy coming from them, others would see them in three dimensions and/or moving parts. There were several instances when many of us had similar experiences or reactions to the diagrams. There were also those that didn't feel anything because the drawings didn't resonate with them.

What will you feel? All, some, or none, of the above, and much more. There will be those of you that are taken far away when you link the drawings up. Some of you will be held transfixed as the two dimensions on the paper become three, form vessels, keys, or entire cities. There are those that may even connect to guides they never knew they had through some of these.

Who is this book for? You. If you were drawn to pick this book up and just can't stop looking at one or more of the pages, if you enjoy sacred geometry work and/or sacred symbols, if you feel the energy coming from the pages as you flip through them, this book is for you.

What should you do with it? Play.

Be sure to let Donna know about your experiences with them. I'm sure she will be delighted to hear them, and the "Thursdays" will, too.

Shannon R. Adams

Reprinted with Permission for noncommercial personal use only. From the Book: Beyond the Code © 2012 Donna Linn

PREFACE

Symbols will become very important in the next few years. They have the ability to employ many layers of information to communicate concepts and information in a very small space, and without any misunderstanding of those concepts. These symbols use color, number, vibration, shape, etc., each piece being another layer of information ready to be accessed by the soul and shared with the body and mind of the person looking at the symbol, to bring the knowledge and healing through for him/her to use.

Symbols can only be understood through the soul and then filtered into the body and mind to use. All we have to do is re-learn how to understand what each layer means and how to use that understanding in our daily life. It requires us to be aware of our soul and how we get information from it to use every day in every situation.

Given the shapes and colors within these drawings, I tapped into geometry, meditation, language, numbers, music, art, dance, and possibly other genres of which I am not even aware. I am sure there is much more to these drawings than I understand, and I would love to know what other people find in them.

Reprinted with Permission for noncommercial personal use only. From the Book: Beyond the Code © 2012 Donna Linn

Reprinted with Permission for noncommercial personal use only. From the Book: Beyond the Code © 2012 Donna Linn

PART ONE

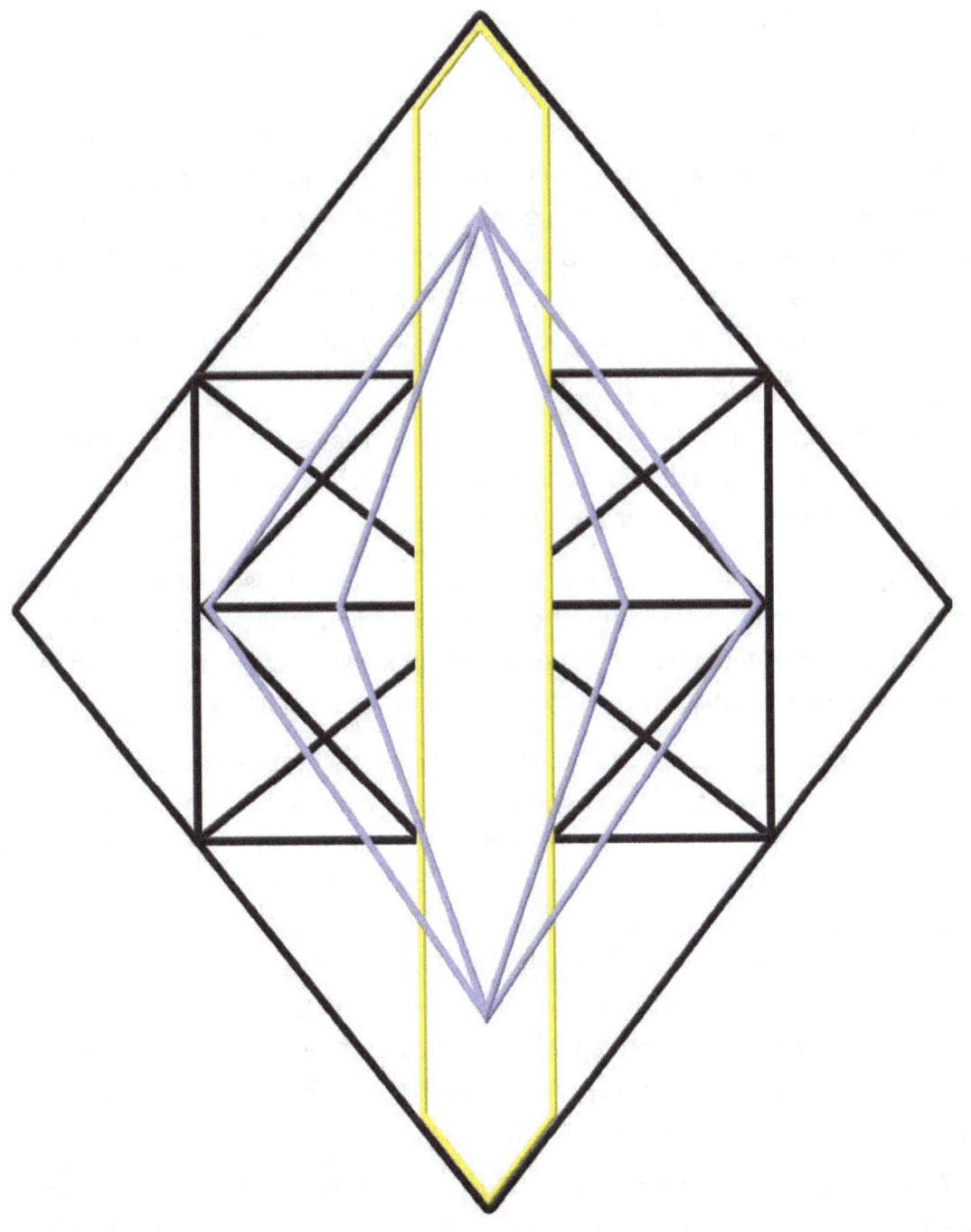

INTRODUCTION

If you are one of those people who can see or feel energy, this book will help you understand just how the energy lines interact with each other and with you. If you don't consciously know, see, feel, or hear energy, you may be surprised that, with these drawings, you are able to tune into one of these modalities—and all of a sudden, you become open to other possibilities and probabilities within these drawings, and the world in general. You become more aware of synchronicities in your life and how life scenarios relate to your higher awareness.

These designs have always been available to initiates of certain mystery schools, but only now are we on earth ready for the knowledge embedded within these designs. They will open long-closed pathways in humans.

The geometric entities gave me these designs for the use of the world. Starting after the numerology patterns (the basis of everything in the world[s]). They began giving the drawings that I had to put down on paper and color. They guided my hand in producing the designs, and always showed me what colors to us

This book is not about words and descriptions of sacred geometric symbols—even though they use sacred geometric symbols, colors, numbers, vibrations and patterns. It is, rather, a chance to use these symbols to reconnect with what the shapes mean to you. Each one has an energy, a form that is different, with different meaning. They are all multidimensional doorways or portals to another part of your Self: different dimensions, different universes, or galaxies. They are intended for individual growth back to the Source. Each person will find his/her individual meanings for these drawings. Some will beckon you to another dimension, another universe, another galaxy. Others will make accessible new pathways for you to follow. Still others will be as a pleasant resting place. Whatever you need, you will receive.

This is powerful sacred geometry. Some of the simplest designs are the most powerful. Each drawing has its own purpose for our third dimensional world. One

Reprinted with Permission for noncommercial personal use only. From the Book: Beyond the Code © 2012 Donna Linn

person will put 2-3 fingers of each hand on specific points of intersecting lines, with one hand being the receiver and the other the grounder. The extra point used by the thumb will be the energy booster. One of these purposes is to look at the energy given by the Geo-matrix entities serving the Creator to give our planet (and the universe[s]) the ability to connect with these higher energies, to help us grow into our understanding of how to use these energies in a conscious way to bring about growth within us all. Esoterically each number and each figure—circle, triangle, square, etc., has a meaning and an energy of its own. All of the diagrams seem to have a specific message to the world at this time. A few they told me. I do not know what that message iwill be for each person.

This is their book, not mine. I was just the vehicle for getting their designs down on paper. Sometimes the drawings came fast, then there would be a pause, then another group would show up. The majority of this happened in the space of about six months, with a few coming earlier and then later as I worked on the book. I had no idea why I was drawing these pictures, just that I needed to get them down on paper.

Each week, I went to what we loosely termed the "Thursdays" group, and I would show the drawings I had made since the last class. This group kept telling me about the energy of the drawings (I called the pictures my "toys"). Each person who played with them had different experiences and different ideas about the meanings. Finally, I got the message that they should not have words. Every person would get what they needed from the drawings—and to tell them what to expect would be limiting that which could come through.

One way to use these drawings is to focus your attention on the different shapes—circles, points, lines, angles, and try to see how they work together, not only for pleasure to the eye, but also the energy within them. Another way is to use them as meditation tools. Turn them upside down, sideways, on an angle. Use two or three together or with the portals, etc. They are on one side only in order to stop the energy of one drawing bleeding into the next. You may need to put an extra sheet of paper or light cardboard under the drawing to stop this bleed-through.

Tapping into this energy is easy. Just put your finger(s) on one or more of the points (intersections) in the drawing. This will put you into the grid. Two or three people can use the same drawing, one being the receiver, one the grounder, and the third as an energy booster. The receiver and grounder each put two-three-four fingers of each hand (depending on the number of points in the drawing) on his/her half of the picture. The energy booster puts one finger somewhere on the design after all the other fingers are down. The receiver and grounder complete a circuit (battery).. The

Reprinted with Permission for noncommercial personal use only. From the Book: Beyond the Code © 2012 Donna Linn

grounder may also be the booster after all fingers are in place. The receiver places his/her fingers first, then the grounder, and finally the booster (or grounder's thumb/finger). These drawings may give you answers to questions—or bring up other questions, show the energy available to you, show you different places, work with your chakras, or just give a pleasant feeling.

While learning how to use these diagrams, the "Thursdays" tried tuning forks, small crystal clusters, other stones, jewelry with healing stones, and different colors under an acetate drawing, or some/all of the above. Each time the energy changed. Even the placement of the fingers on the intersections of lines from one time to another changed what happened.

There is great energy and multidimensionality within each drawing, but it feels different for each person receiving. It seems to give you what you need at your present time, and a hint of the power you have. Messages can come through, music can be heard, places can be visited, possibilities can be seen, additional worlds can be visited. One especially gives a very peaceful feeling for most people, and another one acts like a spaceship "beam me up, Scotty" energy. These drawings are to help make you aware of the greatness of you, and the power you have, to modify experiences through positive life changes.

These drawings were given to me. I am not an artist, nor mathematical at all. But I would sit down at my desk, paper in front of me, and it would just flow. Then, with colored pencils available, my hand would just go to the right color for each area. The first try was always the best. If I tried to remake it, it was never quite as good. Some drawings are very involved, with many different lines; some are very simple. Others, whether complex or simple, have a bigger story to tell. And some of the drawings work together. They are arranged in groups of two, three, four, five, or six. One even has seven in its group. The portals, gateways, transits, accelerators, links, and stand-alones are at the back of the book, because many of them can, and should, be used with more than one set of drawings, or several individual drawings. Just play with them. You will intuitively know which one, or ones, are meant for you at that time—to meditate with, to observe shapes and colors, to hear the music, or see the movement, or whatever else you are led to learn.

After the drawings were mostly finished, in order to understand what I was doing, I started to look at geometry books, sacred geometry books, sacred symbol books. I began to get some idea what I was doing. I still don't understand the mathematics of it: the golden spiral, the golden mean, square root of two, square root of three, square root of five, pi, phi, Fibonacci series of numbers. A 20th Century mathematician, H.

Reprinted with Permission for noncommercial personal use only. From the Book: Beyond the Code © 2012 Donna Linn

S. M. Coxeter, in his book, *Regular Polytypes*, showed how diagrams can have three, four, or more dimensions. I sort-of understood it, but not really—and yet I knew this was what I was tapping into. Modern mathematics also talks about composing a three-dimensional shape and decomposing it into a two-dimensional figure. In some of these drawings, this seems to be what I have done.

I release this book to the world with much trepidation, because I am sure that this was knowledge only allowed to high initiates in the past ages. But I also know that now is the time for anyone who wants to, to become better acquainted with them, and use the knowledge stored in these drawings to become more aware of his/her potential and inner greatness.

EXPLANATION

Esoterically each number, color, and figure (circle, triangle, square, etc.) has a meaning. All the diagrams seem to have a specific message to the world at this time. A few they told me, most I do not know what that message is. I was given the privilege of putting them down on paper for all to use.

All the numbers that the Ancients used in their buildings, temples, and pyramids, fit a particular sequence of numbers and geometric points, lines, connected lines with specific angles. Those shapes and angles the Ancients used in construction seem to take the numbers of the earth—circumference, diameter, radius, distance to the sun and moon, distance to certain stars and planets. Many of the buildings have lines and angles that are the same in different parts of the world, at roughly the same time-periods. These numbers, as straight lines, are connected to form a particular geometrical shape seemingly even before the ancient Egyptian priests. Whereever the information came from, it seems to be very ancient—possibly at the time of the forming of the planet—or brought here from another place.

How did the builders get the information? Was it given to initiates in the mystery school? Was it handed down from somewhere else? The more we learn, the more questions for which we have no answers. This is only a small portion of the Ancients' knowledge that they left for us in the form of stone.

Many of these figures make music, but I don't know enough about music to be able to hear it. A friend of mine has a musician partner who looked at some of the designs. He is an intuitive musician who does not read notes, but he not only heard the music, but was able to record it. It was an amazing experience to hear the music he heard in the diagrams. Another friend used a few of the drawings during a very trying time in her life. She came back several weeks later and said they had changed her perceptions and perspective about the problem.

Reprinted with Permission for noncommercial personal use only. From the Book: Beyond the Code © 2012 Donna Linn

There is also language within these drawings. It is a sacred language known very many, many years ago. I only know it is there but cannot decipher it. The drawings are not only geometry, but sacred geometry and some people can take pictures of buildings and place these drawings in overlays to see the connections. In art, the human body is seen in perfected ratios between parts of the body to describe what we call beautiful. There are many other patterns, many other aspects, to each drawing. I have just skimmed the surface of the knowledge that is beginning to be shown to the world at this time.

I also know that all my drawings show energy and energy patterns waiting for you to tap into. Some are portals to higher places, some are gateways, some are transits, some are links to other pictures, some are to balance chakras, and some are just to help you cope with everyday challenges. Let them talk to you. Ask questions. You will get answers—or more questions. Skip around. Don't necessarily go page by page, although that is one way to do it. Use it as a flip book until you find a picture, or pictures, to which you are attracted. Each one has many different aspects and help. You will be drawn to those that you need.

DISCUSSION

Geometry is the branch of mathematics that measures and shows relationships between points, lines, angles, surfaces, and faces, whether plane figures (points and lines) or solid figures (points and lines plus surfaces and faces in a three [or more] dimensional figure). The name comes from the Greek word (geometrein) which means to measure, geo (land) and metron (measure). Sacred Geometry is the use of these figures in the most beautiful proportions and ratios using the golden mean, golden spiral, etc., square roots of two, three and five, phi, pi, and Fibonacci numbers.

From my limited understanding of geometry, and from reading scientific and metaphysical sources, this is what I have come to believe true for each shape, number, and color in my drawings.

1. CIRCLE/SPHERE

Many objects can make a circle: compass, protractor, anything that is round, or freehand. All of these still have the same energy. Whether it is a single circle, two interlocking circles, whatever, they have the same characteristics—point, radius, diameter, curved edge, and circumference.

You can start anywhere on its edge (circumference) and continue all the way around. It has constant width and distance around the surface. Any point on the circle is equidistant from the fixed point in the center. The center point attracts all the circumference energy (by way of the diameter or radii) back to the center so that the energy can project outward. The point used in making the circle is the core of the circle's power and that power radiates to any point or points on the circumference through the center. No matter how many ways you divide the circle, the energy always comes back to the center point.

The circle is the zero of both no-thing, and possibilities/probabilities for everything. The points of the circle circumference are lessons you have to learn at some point in your incarnations on this planet or others, or in other dimensions. All must be finished before getting off the karmic wheel and going back to the Source.

Reprinted with Permission for noncommercial personal use only. From the Book: Beyond the Code © 2012 Donna Linn

We find the circle in nature, both flat and in its three-dimensional solid form, a sphere. The sphere is the primordial soup of creation where all possibilities exist. It represents the One, the All, from which all things are born. It is also a traditional symbol of heaven, of wholeness, of unity and one of the original shapes. The sphere is the dimensional shape of the earth, of the universe.

When circles are inter-connected, there is a different energy in that inter-connected space. It is not a circular form anymore. The interconnected part takes energy from both circles and changes it to accommodate a different energy. Depending on the size and shape of the interconnected circles (although not a circle itself), the wavelengths (energy) will be different, because the arcs are different dimensions of the original circles. The area inside shows how much of each circle energy is available to be changed.

Putting two circles together by using a point on the first circle circumference and making an equal arc in the second circle will give you what is called the *vesica pisces*. Most other geometric forms can be constructed in this area.

When circles intertwine as in the flower of life, the design given to many, many cultures, the energy is only one universe. If seen three-dimensionally, that same design shows not only one universe, but many more, intertwined for the betterment of all the universes. It is working together for the greatest good of everyone in all the universes—brotherhood at its best.

Half circles have their own energy. It is not the same as if it were a whole circle. Using the diameter as a break in the circle gives the energy a block so that it can only manifest half of its original energy or wavelength. Therefore, it concentrates on coming/going through the center point. The half circle shows the outer lesson, and all indications for growth and understanding. The radius gives direction from the center of the circle to the way out for expression.

Less than half a circle points directly to the center of the circle and the energy comes in or goes out very strongly, almost like a funnel. If the energy is coming in, it disperses to each part equally. If the energy is going out, it generates more force by taking the energy of the arc and pouring it toward the point within the partial circle.

The elongated shape of the circle (oval) has a slightly different energy than that of the circle. The energy is still somewhat circular, but it takes longer to get all the way around the oval. Within an oval, there are short bursts of energy and then long bursts of energy. The energy will differ according to the place on the oval measured.

Reprinted with Permission for noncommercial personal use only. From the Book: Beyond the Code © 2012 Donna Linn

2. LINES

We classify a line as straight between two points. It is labeled a straight-line segment because the points stop it at both ends. Lines are in one dimension only. But with other points which limit it size, it shows many possibilities. By using points, we limit the distance we can see or connect with that energy. It is, in its infinity, a straight line to the All. If vertical, the line represents the number one which in numerology means self, leadership, and the "I Am".

We need two points to stop the straight line. The two in numerology signifies duality and balance. Two is our world of polarity—right and wrong, good and bad, black and white. The line segment is an essential shape with which to make all other geometric figures except the circle, (zero—no thing or all possibilities), and therefore, reflects and refines the polarity of how we see the world.

3. TRIANGLE/PYRAMID

A triangle uses three connected straight-line segments to make a three-sided polygon, or a closed plane figure. Triangles are classified by size of angle (more than 90 degrees—obtuse, less than 90 degrees-acute, 90 degrees-right) and by number of sides equal (3 sides equal-equilateral, 2 sides equal-isosceles, no sides equal-scalene). You will usually find triangles together or inside/outside other shapes.B

The triangle is used in our world to delineate three related subjects or concepts. It is considered by some as two sides of a duality (black, white) with the third side showing the solution or resolution of that duality (shades of gray).

When teaching the use of color in art, we use three interconnected circles to show the relationship of one color to another. In science classes, atoms have three parts—protons, electrons, and neutrons. Another unit usually involves animals/insects with three body parts—head, body, tail or equivalent. If you look at our life, we see three stages—birth, growth, death. Our government has three parts---Congressional, Executive, and Judicial. Metaphysically, we speak of body, mind, and spirit. In Geometry, we use a ruler, compass, pencil/paper to construct all the figures—although now the computer does most of that work for us. Writing classes teach older children about thesis, antithesis, and synthesis, while younger children learn beginning, middle, and end. Music has thirds as combinations of notes.

The solid form of the triangle is a pyramid. It was constructed through the world in eons past. We are most familiar with the three sided and triangle base and four sided and square (or rectangle) base of the pyramids of the world. These have been the primary shape seen in our world for the past millennia of human experience. Atlantis, ancient Egypt, South America, Bosnia, etc., used the pyramid shape because it could

Reprinted with Permission for noncommercial personal use only. From the Book: Beyond the Code © 2012 Donna Linn

generate spiral energy and send it skyward. In other times and places, there may be pyramids with a different number of sides and a different looking base—perhaps a pentagon, hexagon, octagon, or other. Since we have not seen these physically, we assume they do not exist. But do they exist in other dimensions, or in other universes? We do not know. All pyramids—no matter how many sides—are energy makers and conduits— transmitters and receivers.

We are not sure how they initiated this energy flow, but they seem to have had some sort of primitive (to us) battery. When the point reaches toward the sky, it sends spiraling energy up, and when the point reaches down, it sends spiraling energy down toward the Earth. Putting two or more triangles together will enhance the ability to generate this spiral energy and send it both ways at the same time (almost looks like DNA). They seem also to have been utilized as a repository for knowledge to be opened (learned) at the appropriate time in late years.

The meaning of three in numerology is association, groups and creativity. We assume groups of people constructed the pyramids. The building of the pyramid shape with such large rocks had to have used much creativity on someone's part.

Two triangles together make a diamond. The three-dimensional diamond shows all the lessons we need to learn—or have learned—within this or all incarnations. The diamond in the diagrams can put you in touch with, and bring forward for use in this lifetime, previous learnings—or show you what else you have to learn.

4. SQUARE/CUBE

A square is a plane figure of four equal sides and four equal angles and is classified as a regular four-sided plane polygon. In Latin, *quadrum* means square. It is not identical to a rectangle. A rectangle has four straight sides and four equal angles, but the adjacent sides are not the same size.

Four is associated in our world with four directions (North, South, East, West), four seasons (spring, summer, autumn, winter), four elements (air, water, earth, fire) and four blood types (A, B, AB, O). The square also has lines that can be treated as two sets of polarities working together.

The cube is the three-dimensional form of a square. It is a regular solid having six congruent square faces. Cube comes from the Greek word *kubos* and Latin word *cubus*. It is a solid having six plane square faces, with right angles on all corners and same size sides. A cube is three-dimensional, solid and durable. The four in numerology means building solid foundations, and the cube portrays this very well.

Reprinted with Permission for noncommercial personal use only. From the Book: Beyond the Code © 2012 Donna Linn

5. PENTAGON

A pentagon is a five-sided polygon. It has five same size sides and five same size interior angles. It is a symbol of light and the mystical center of the universe. The pentagonal star is a symbol of man, of excellence. Music has fifths and five black keys in an octave. We have five appendages on each hand and each foot. Our nickel is worth five cents. We have five accepted senses (seeing, hearing, smelling, tasting, touching), and five virtues (love, wisdom, truth, justice, kindness). The numerology of five is change, freedom, and flexibility.

6. HEXAGON

A hexagonal polygon, also called a closed plane figure, has six equal sides and six equal interior angles. Hexagon comes from the Greek words *hexa* meaning six and *gonos* meaning angles. Hexagonal patterns include the flower of life mandala, and some quilt patterns. It can also be described at interlaced double triangles. Quartz crystals are the three-dimensional shape of a hexagon.

The hexagon can be made into the 12 sided, 24 sided, 30 sided, and 60 sided polygons. The 12-sided polygon name comes from the Greek word *dodeka*. The twelve-sided polygon is useful in astrology as a template for the twelve houses and the twelve zodiac signs. It also indicates the twelve months of the year and can be divided into the four seasons. It equates to four equilateral triangles, two hexagons, or a twelve-pointed star. There are also twelve-sided dice, one octave of black and white keys on a piano, a dozen, sixty seconds in a minute, sixty minutes in an hour, twenty-four hours in a day.

The six-sided hexagon resonates to the six of responsibility, service, and time in our world.

7. HEPTAGON/SEPTAGON

This is a polygon with seven equal sides and angles. It is a figure that we can create closely, but not completely accurately, within the *vesica piscis*. *Hepta* is from the Greek word for seven, while in Latin seven is *septa*, hence the two different names. One octave of white notes on a piano numbers seven. Music also has sevenths. In medieval times, alchemy had seven metals and seven planets. The Christian religion has six days of creation and one day of rest, and there are seven days in our week.

In numerology, seven means spiritual opening and spiritual awareness.

8. OCTOGON

Octo is the Greek word for eight. It is a regular closed figure with all sides and all angles equal. It can be revealed by interlacing two squares.

The Chinese used the double square (4 + 4) to show their medicinal concepts of hot and cold, wet and dry, as well as earth, air, fire, and water. Within each of these lines, they also explained the four kinds of seasonal diseases. The Chinese I Ching is also predicated on trigrams using six lines and sixty-four combinations of yin and yang.

The numerological meaning for eight is using spiritual principles in life and business. It builds upon the two interlaced squares (4) of solid foundations.

9. NONEGON

The nine-sided figure is a polygon composed of three separate intertwined triangles and can also be a nine-pointed star. The nine in numerology is considered the highest point of completeness. It is a completion and review of all lessons learned within that particular block of learning. The nine as a single digit number is the highest digit in our base ten number system, with zero meaning no thing or holding place value.

10. DECAGON

A decagon is a ten-sided polygon. In numerology, the ten is a new beginning on a higher level. It is a twice pentagon. The foundation of our money system is ten—one dime equals ten pennies or two nickels, ten dimes equal one dollar. We have ten fingers and ten toes.

11. SPIRAL

The spiral shows moving energy and unites Creation with Self in an upward or downward circular flow of balance. It is visible harmony in motion, a sign of growth and change.

There are two types of spirals—the Golden Spiral and the Archimedean spiral. The Golden Spiral, as I understand it, starts in the center and spirals out, according to the Fibonacci sequence of numbers and ratios. The Archimedes spiral starts in the center and grows at a fixed rate with the spiral moving around itself similar to a water hose. We see spirals in screws and in DNA.

Reprinted with Permission for noncommercial personal use only. From the Book: Beyond the Code © 2012 Donna Linn

12. COLORS

Even though I did not consciously choose which colors to use and was guided as to which color to use for each circle or line in the drawings, this is what each color means to me.

The major colors:

>   Red—physical, energy
>
>   Yellow—students, intelligence
>
>   Orange—blending of physical and soul, of red (energy) and gold (sunshine)
>
>   Green—emotional, feelings
>
>   Blue—mental, mind
>
>   Purple—spiritual, higher awareness
>
>   Silver—our cord to Above
>
>   Gold—highest color available to bring to earth, the color of the "I AM" and our Soul

The pastels:

>   Pink—unconditional love
>
>   Light blue—highest mental
>
>   Light green—highest emotional
>
>   Lavender—highest spiritual

13. MISCELLANEOUS

In the beginning and end of the book are pages with nothing on them. This signifies where we came from, where we were, and are, going. The second page and the next to last page contains one small point (center of page) from which everything else is conceptualized. The third page and the third from the last is an eye watching everything that was created or that transpires within the worlds and our lives.

14. CONCLUSION

Within each of the following drawings, you may find one circle, many circles, half circles, and circles divided into triangles, squares, pentagons, hexagons, octagons, or

Reprinted with Permission for noncommercial personal use only. From the Book: Beyond the Code © 2012 Donna Linn

other shapes. Or each shape may stand alone with lines within that shape. Just become one with the drawing and take its message for you. They are all multi-dimensional with many facets of meaning. They will open doorways you suspected were there, or even had no idea they were there. The pictures are in sets of two to six, in my order, but many can be utilized in a different order, or by themselves. I know that my drawings hold energy waiting for you to tap into. Let them talk to you. Ask questions. **You will get what you need at that time, as will everyone else that uses the same drawing—but not necessarily the same information as you.**

Play with them. Vision with them if you so choose. You will find that things start to happen if you are open enough to observe synchronicities within your everyday life. There are no words or explanations for each drawing so that each person will get the meaning needed for him/her-self, and not have a preconceived notion of what will happen.

Enjoy!

**Please put a piece of paper or a light weight cardboard behind the drawing at which you are looking. This will reduce the energy bleed-through from the next drawing or drawings.

To keep the price down, the paper chosen was too thin to keep this bleed-through from happening.

PART TWO

**This page is intentionally left blank.
It shows possibilities and probabilities not yet conceptualized or manifested.**

The beginning of everything.

●

Watching, observing

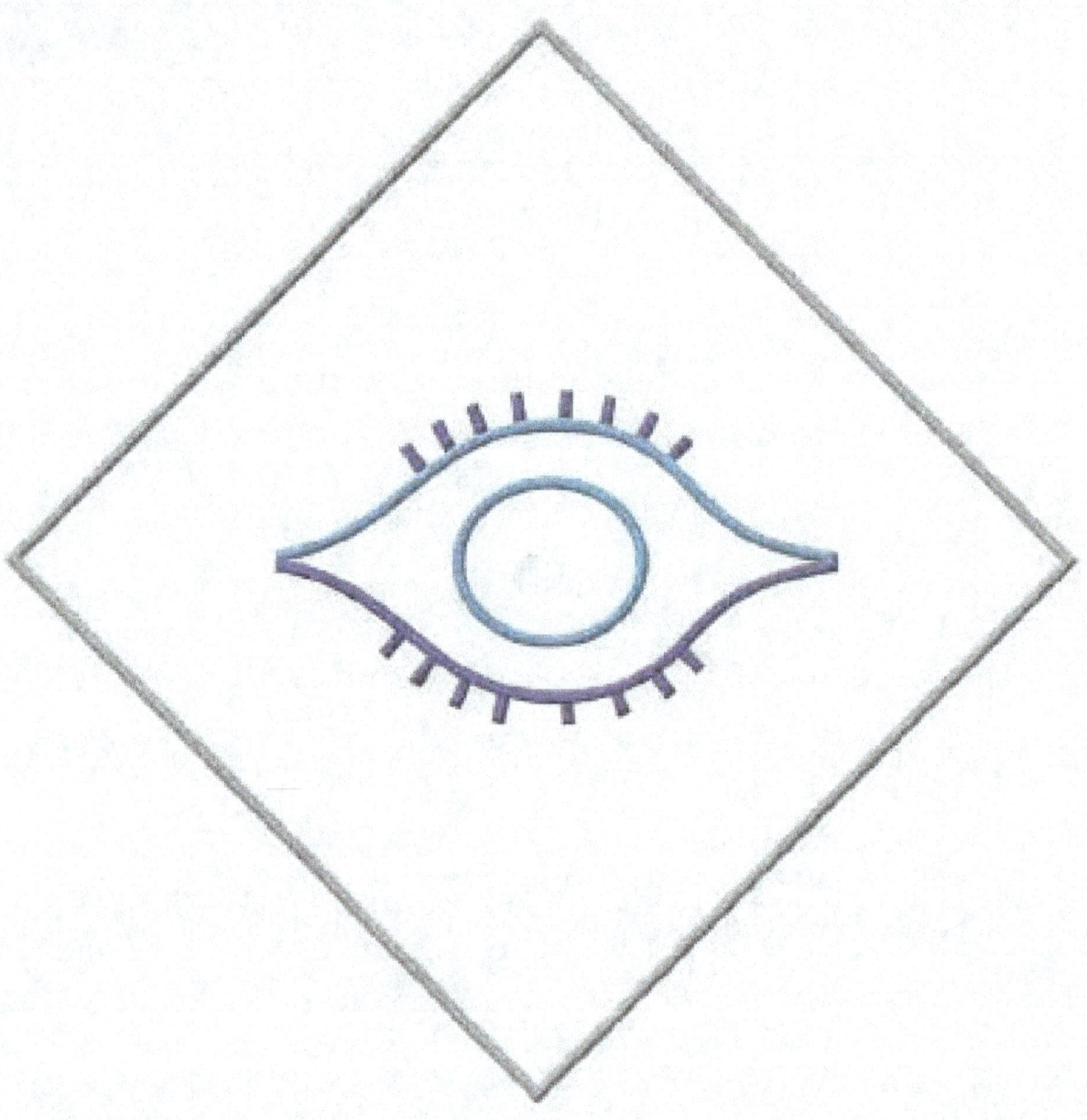

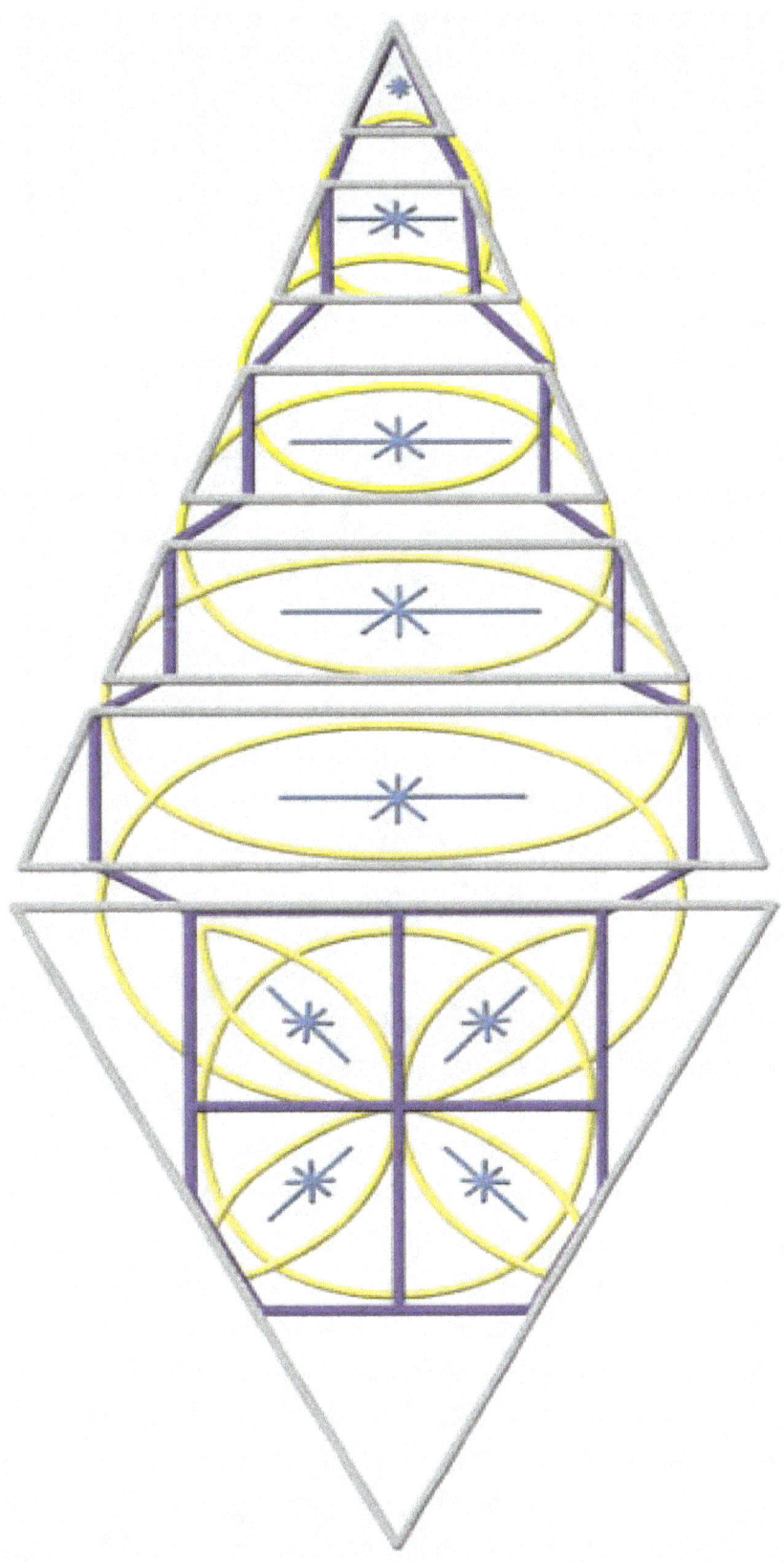

A-1

A-2

Beyond the Code

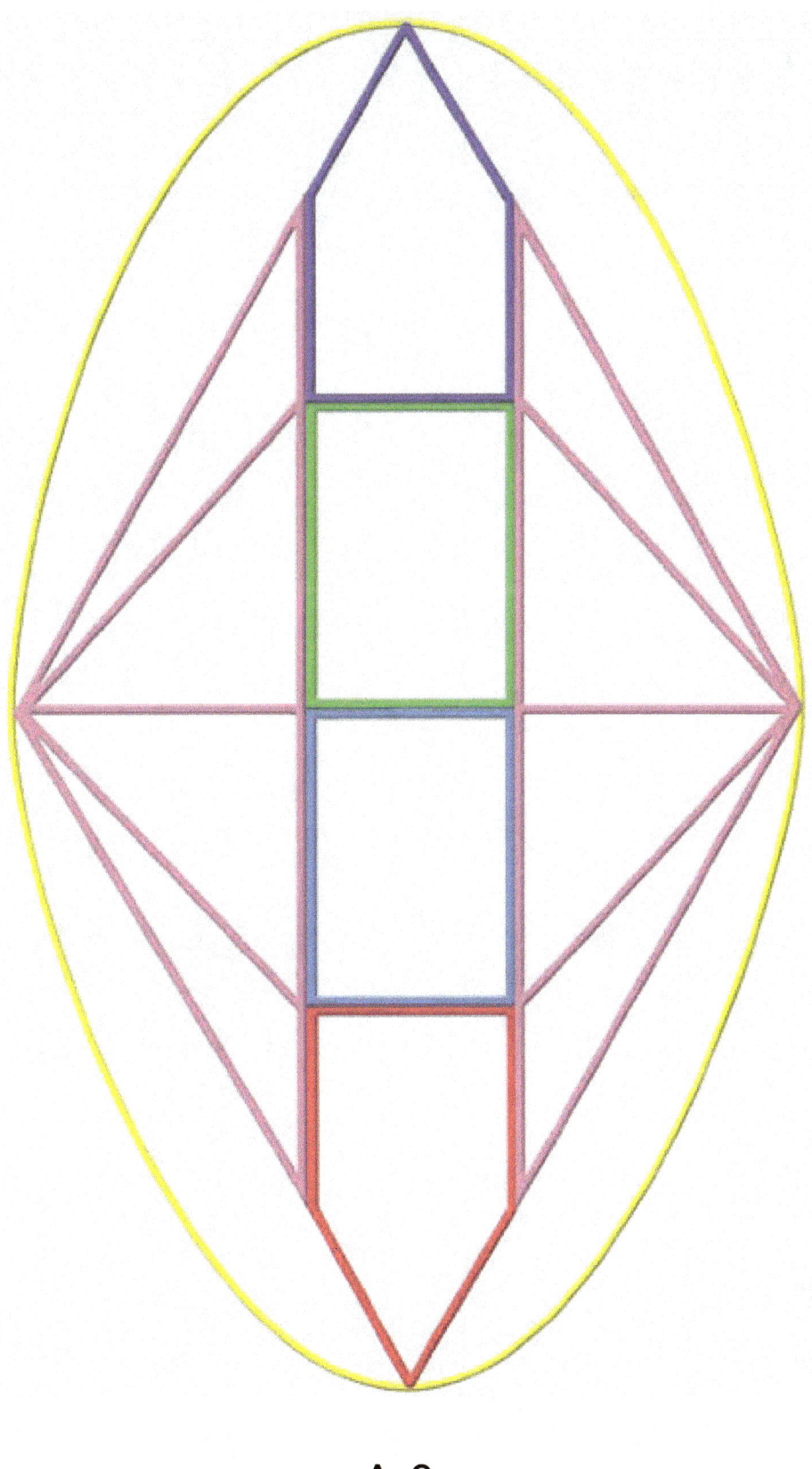

A-3

Beyond the Code

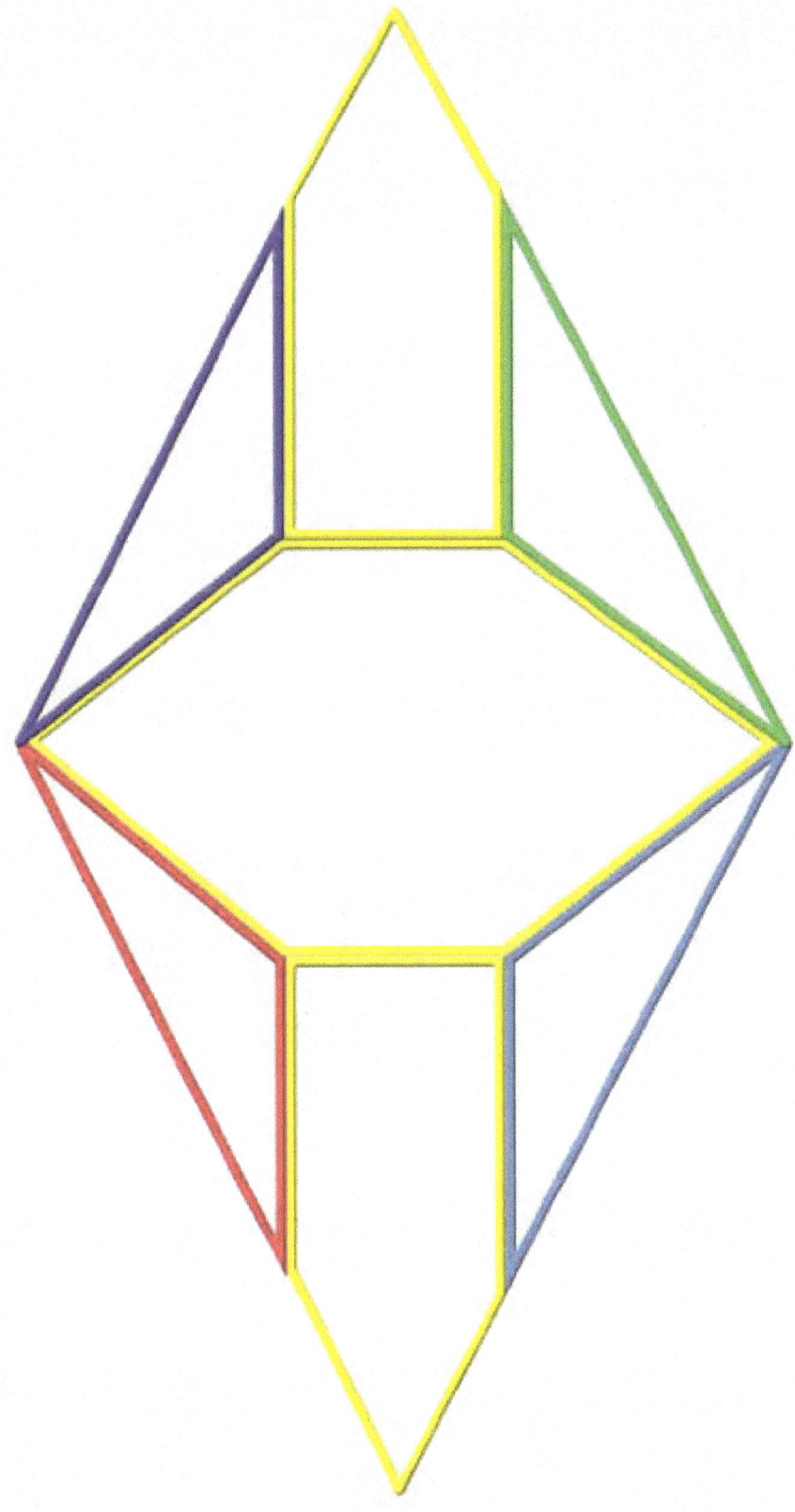

B-1

B-2

B-3

C-1

C-2

C-3

Reprinted with Permission for noncommercial personal use only. From the Book: Beyond the Code © 2012 Donna Linn

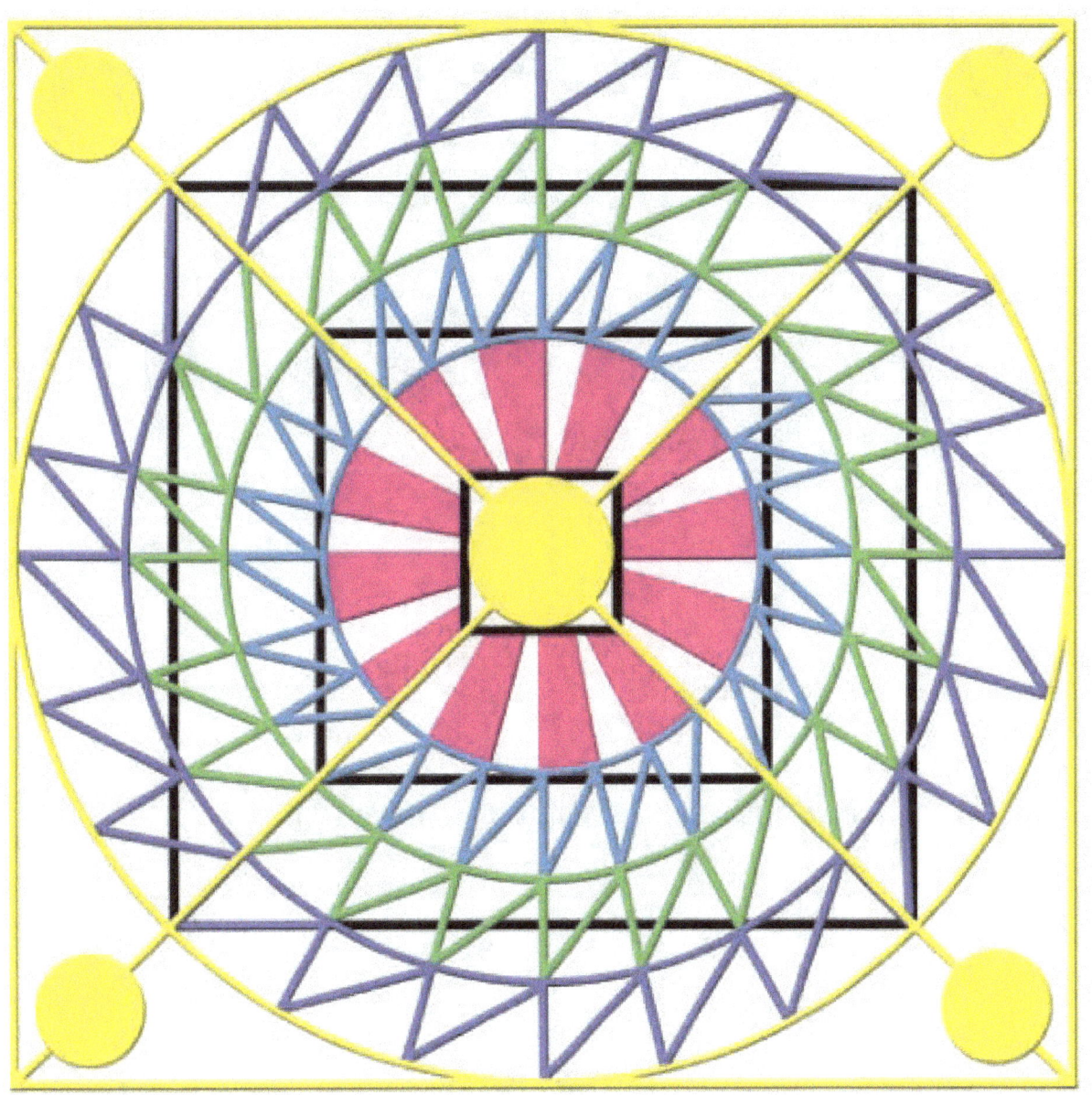

C-4

C-5

D-1

D-2

Beyond the Code

D-3

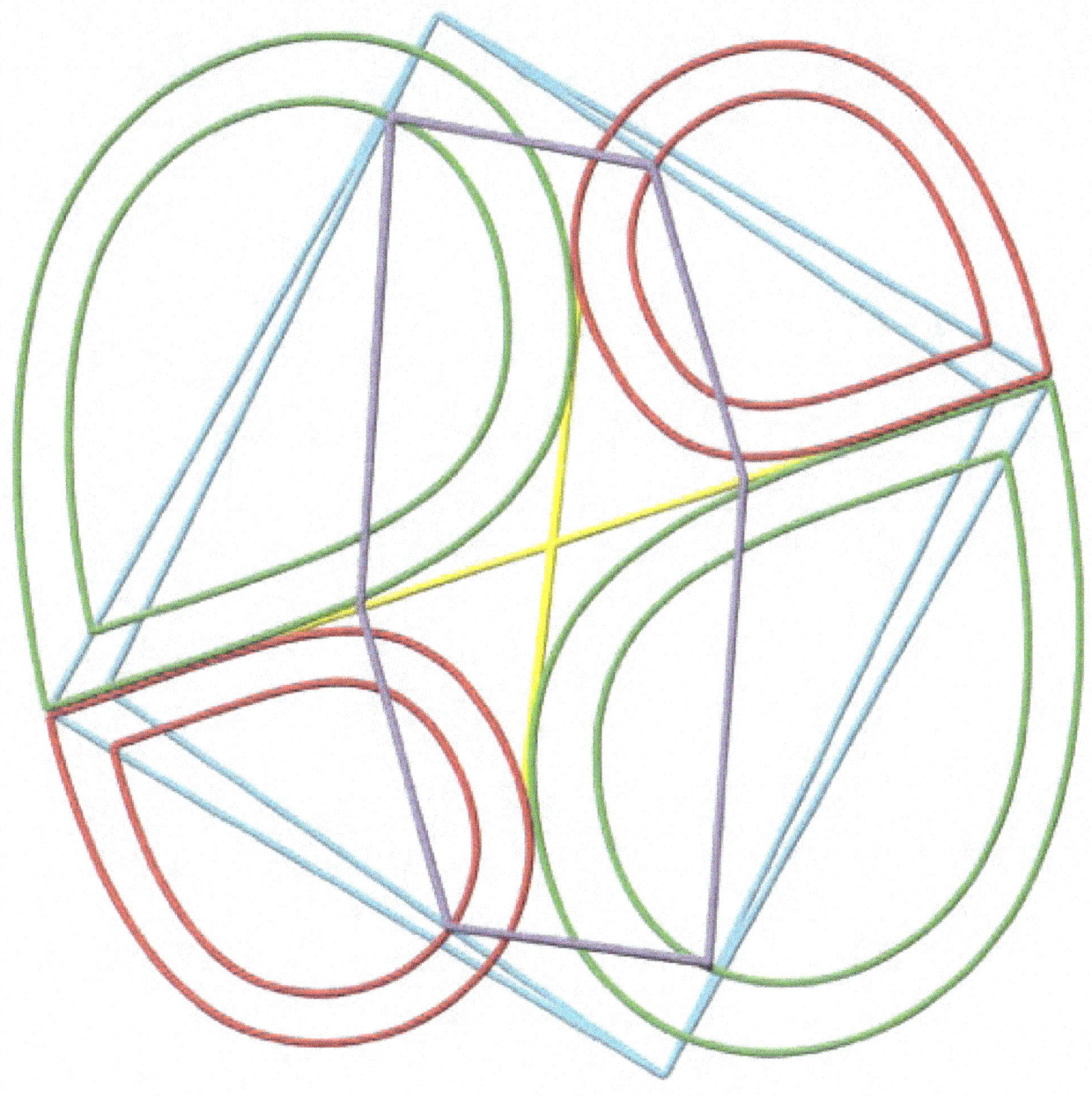

D-4

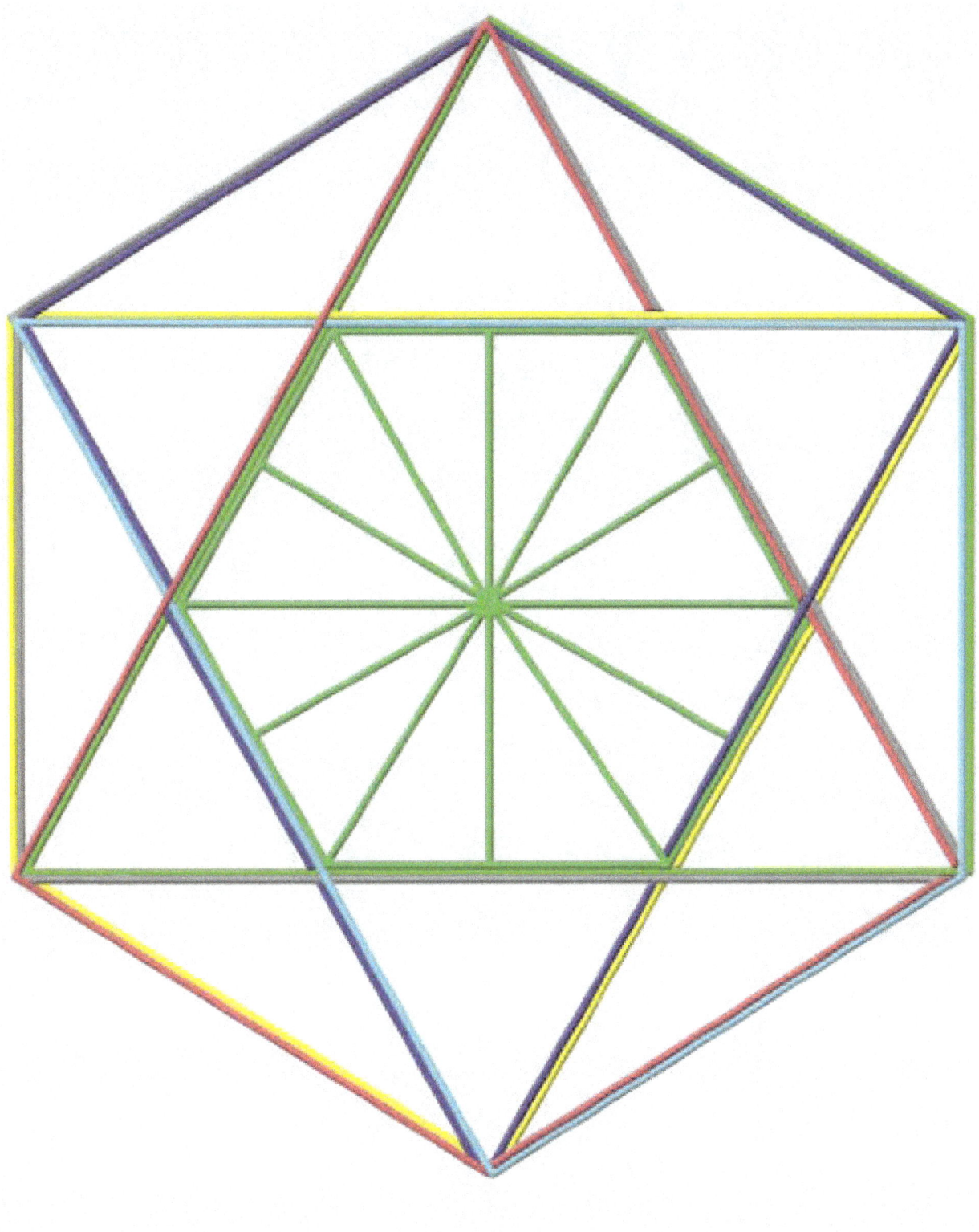

E-1

Beyond the Code

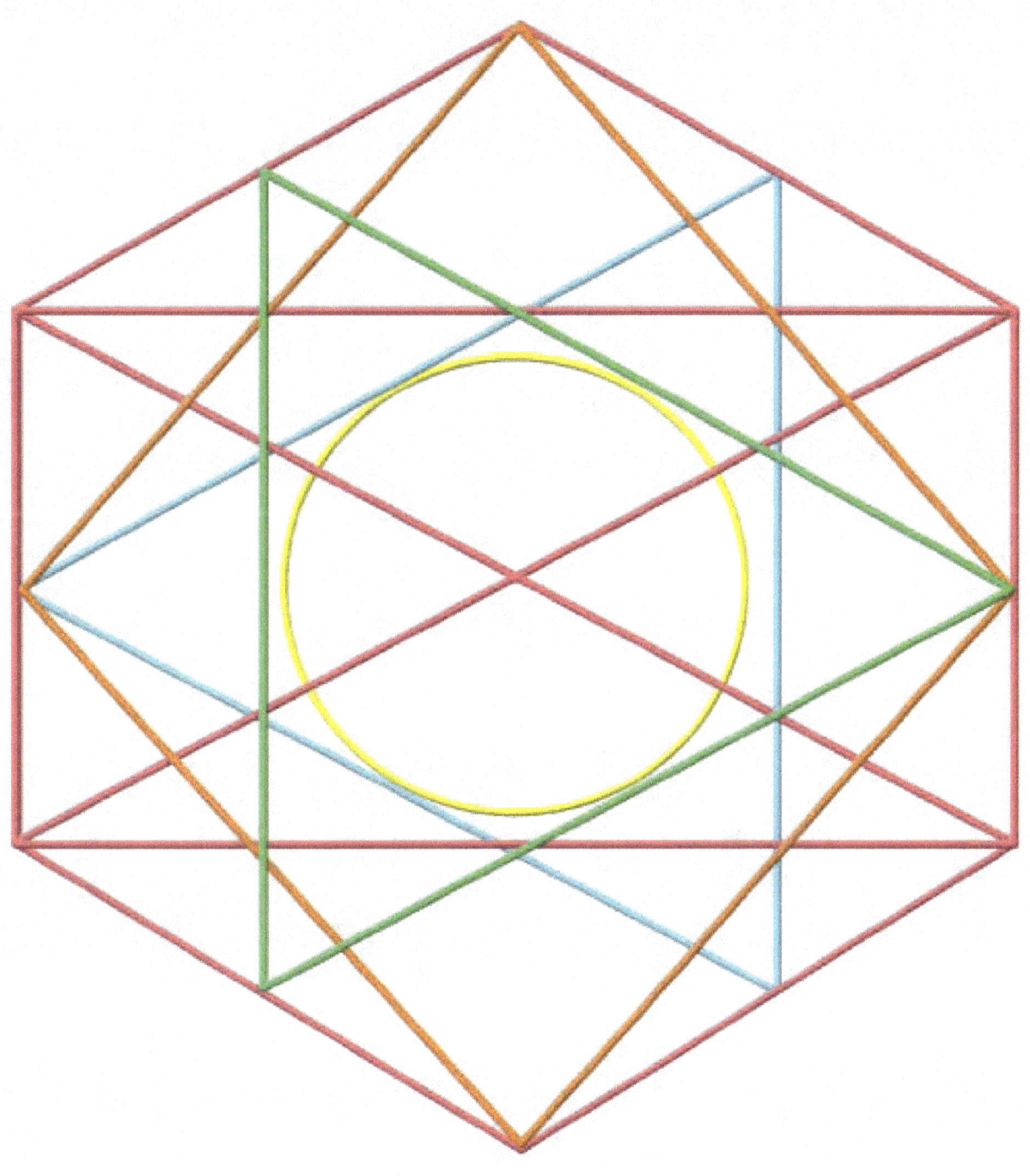

E-2

Beyond the Code

E-3

E-4

Beyond the Code

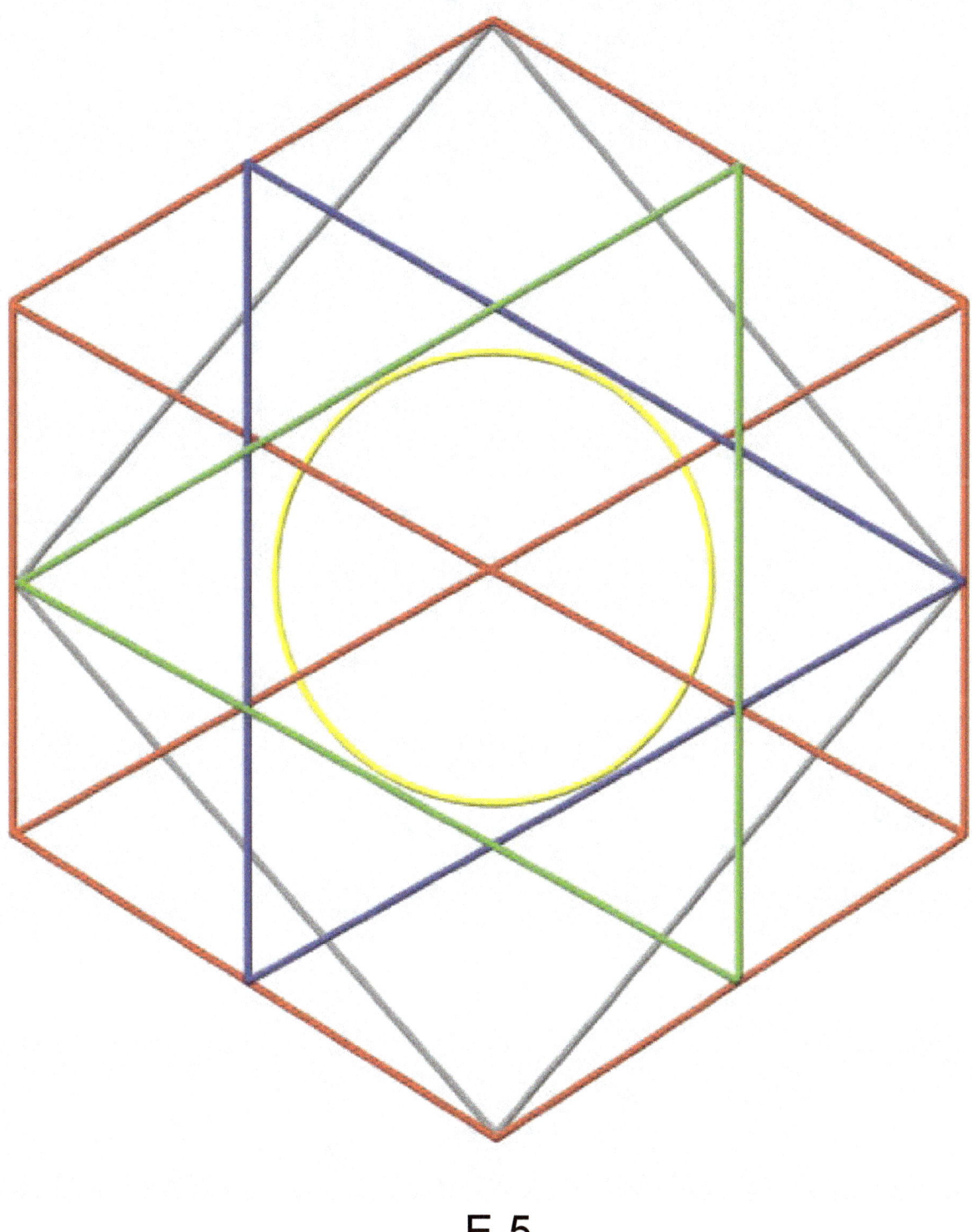

E-5

Beyond the Code

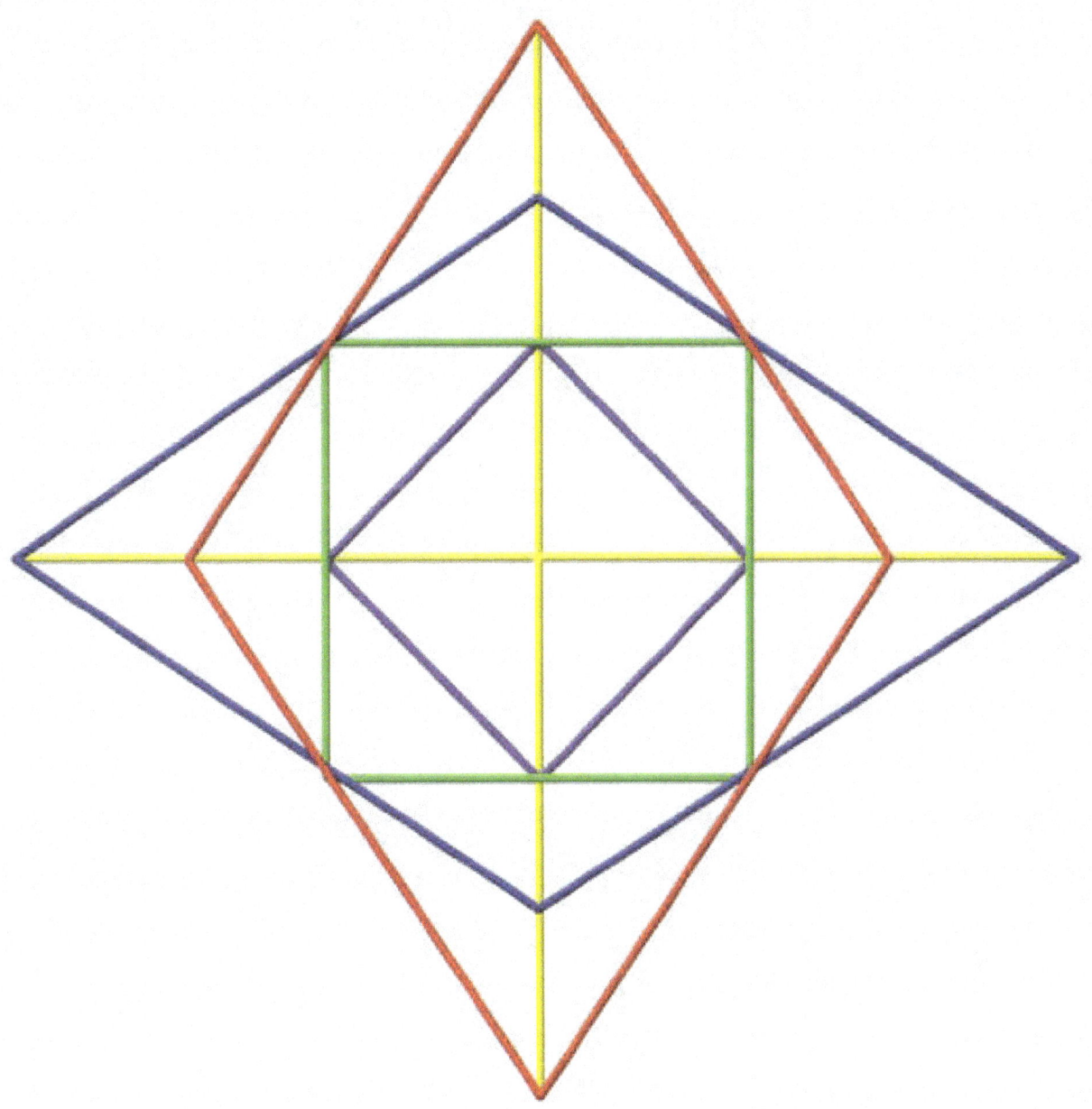

F-1

Beyond the Code

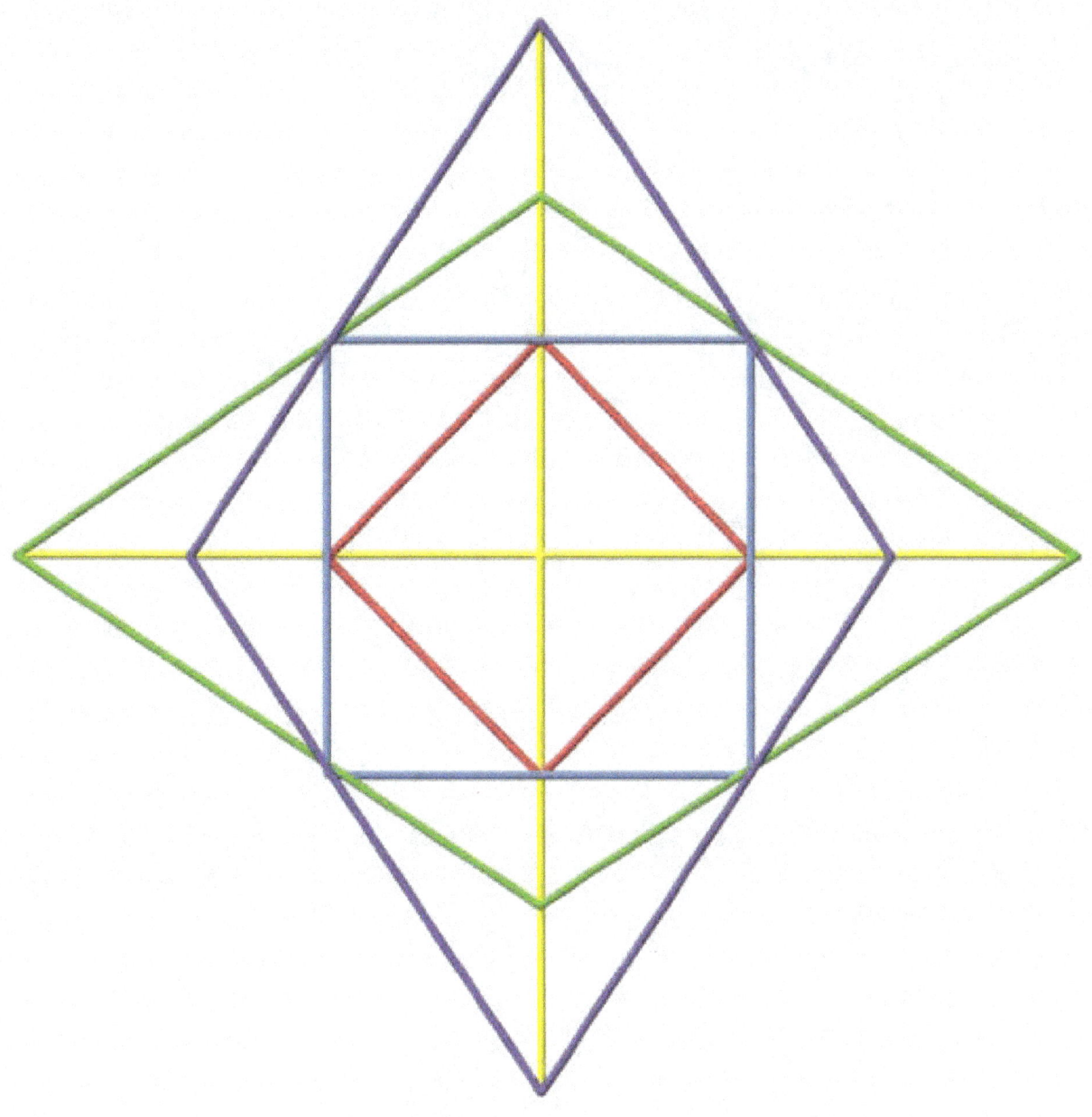

F-2

F-3

Beyond the Code

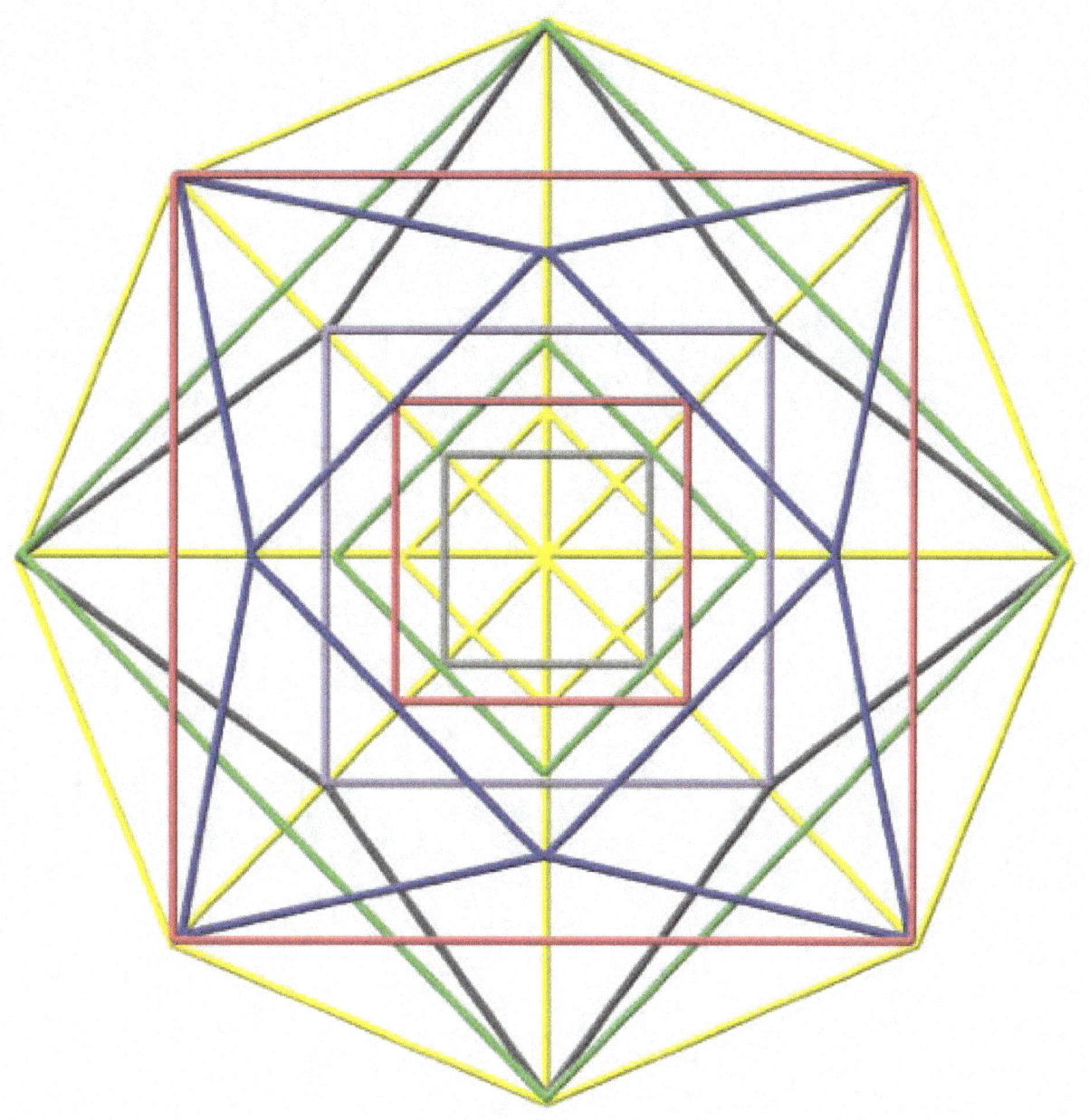

F-4

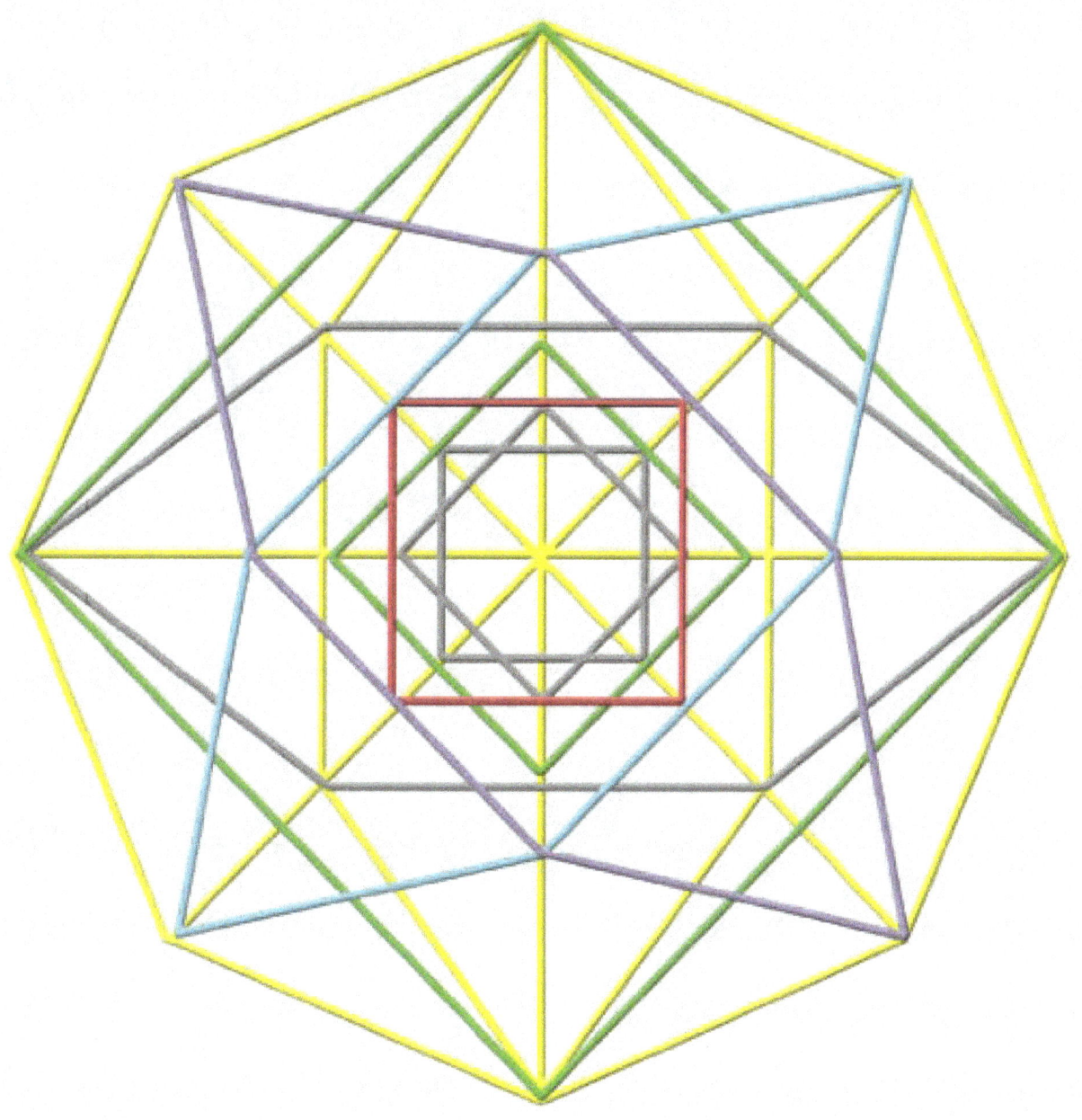

F-5

Beyond the Code

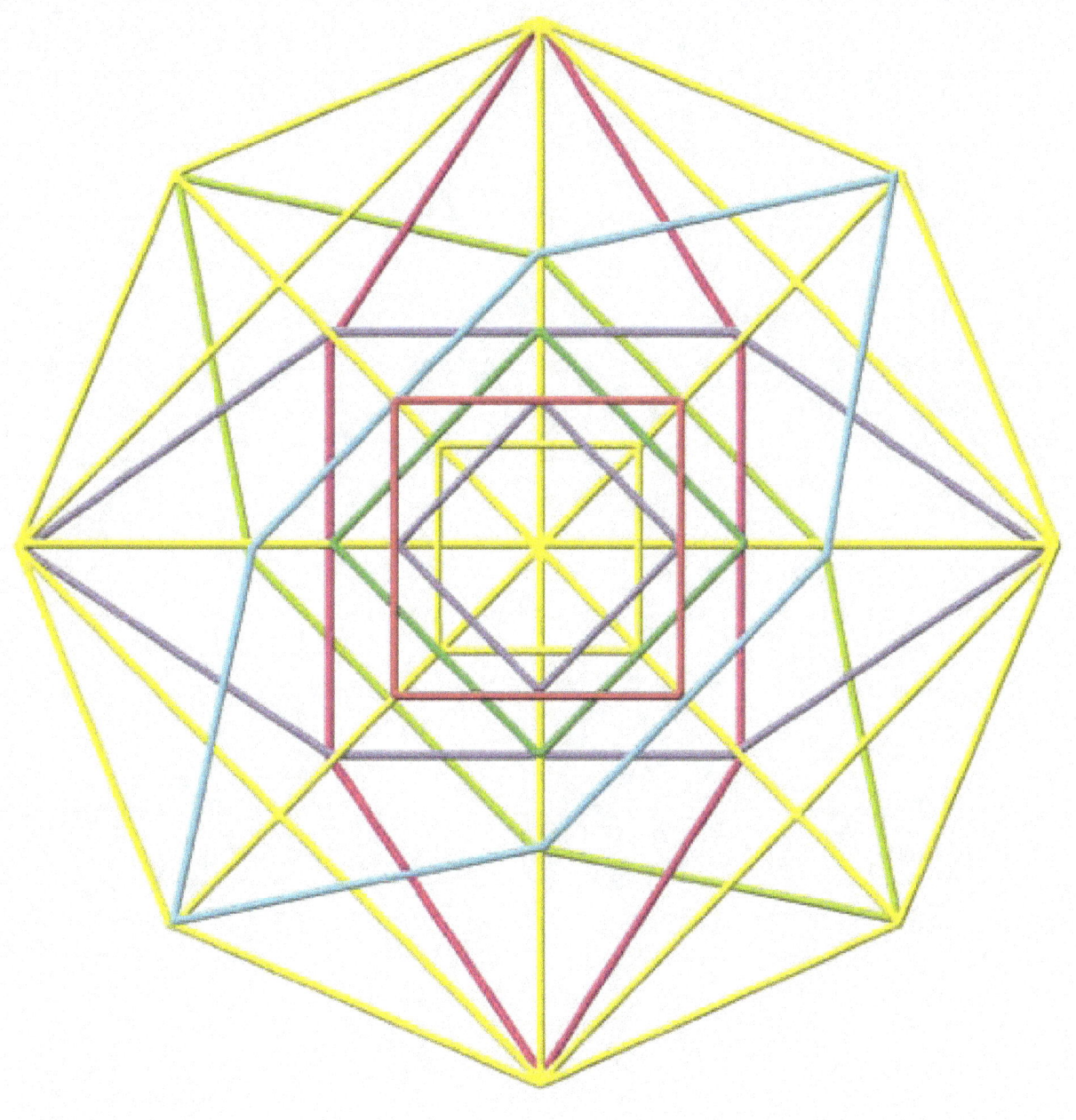

F-6

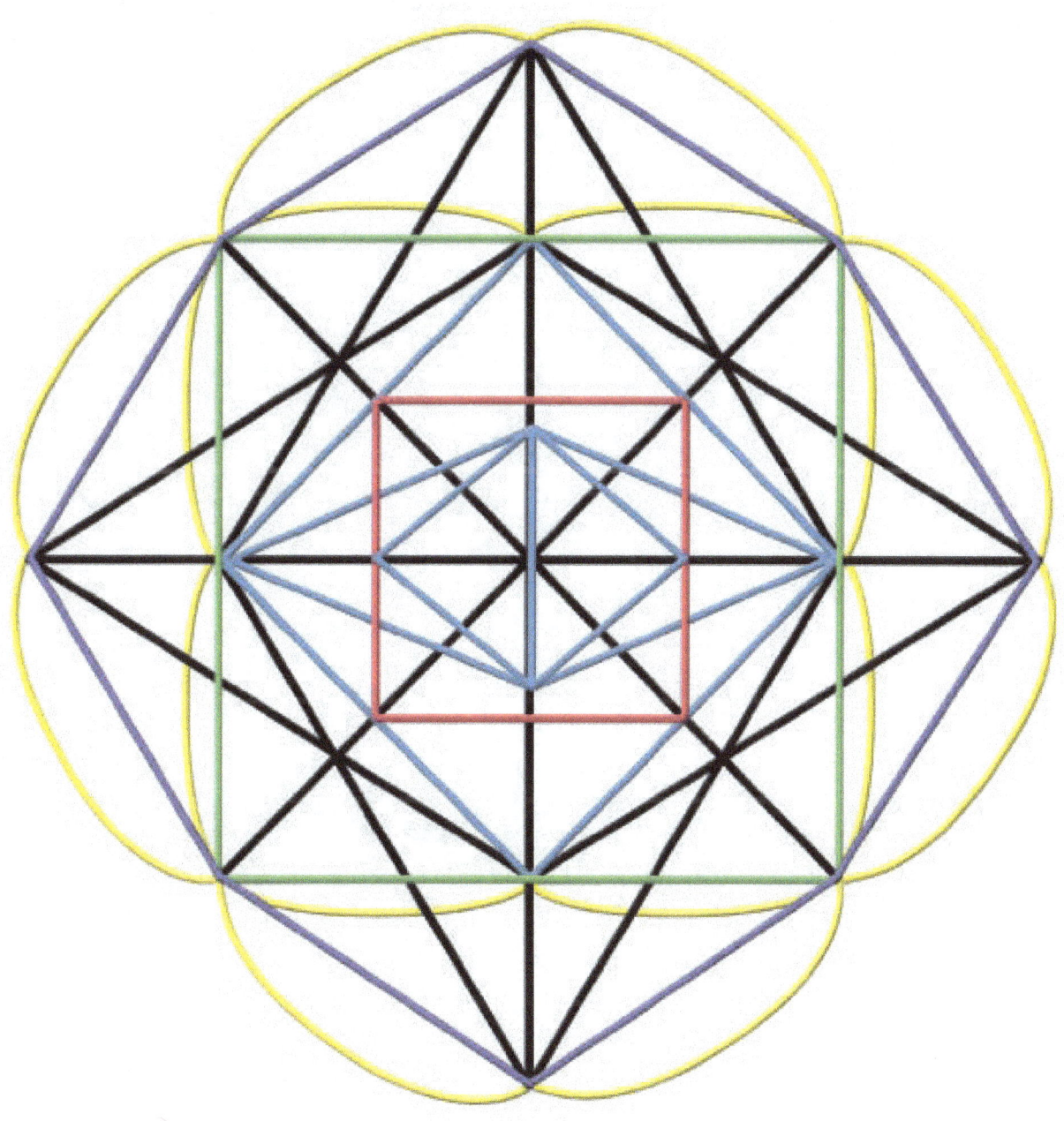

G-1

Reprinted with Permission for noncommercial personal use only. From the Book: Beyond the Code © 2012 Donna Linn

Beyond the Code

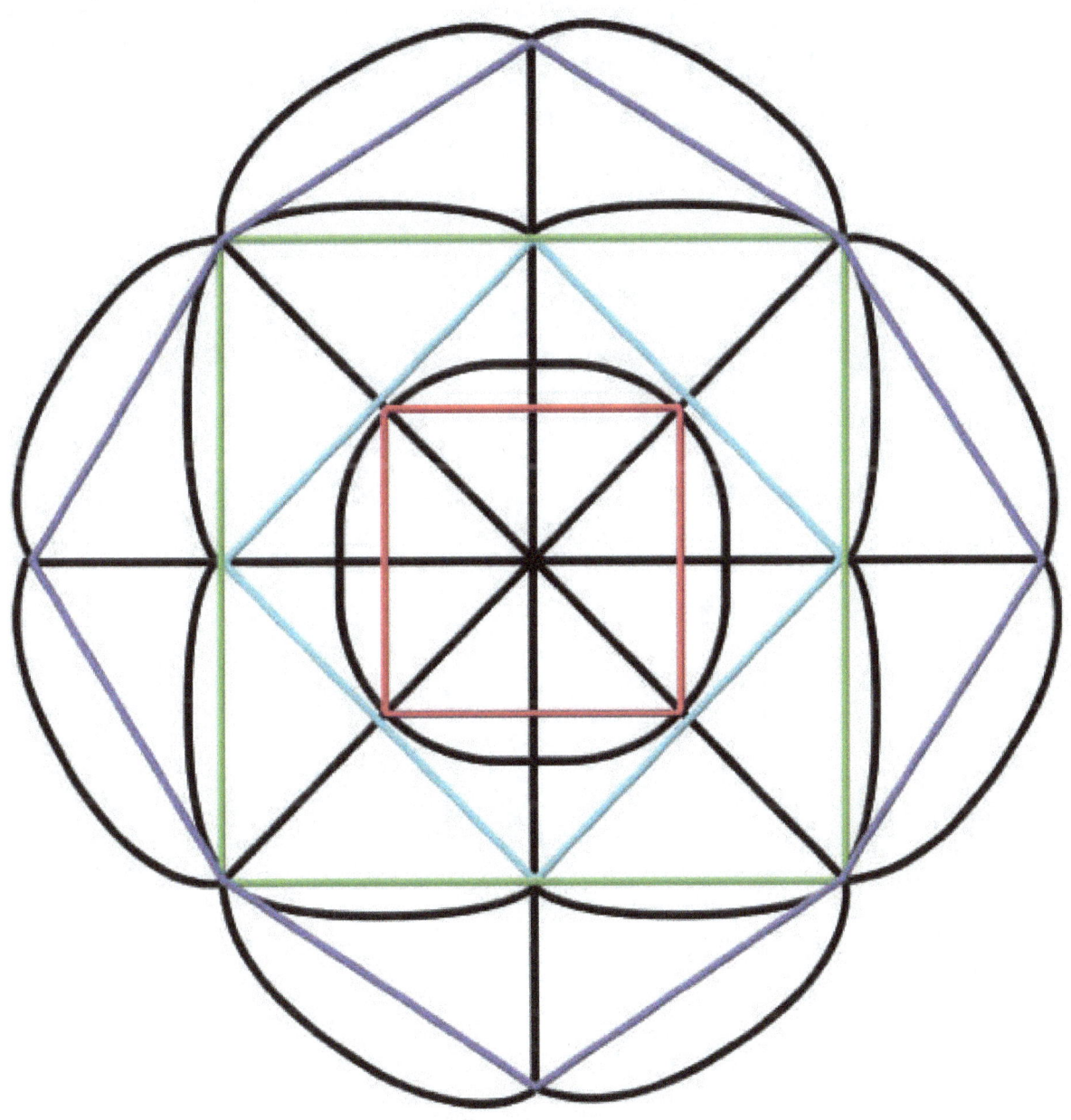

G-2

Beyond the Code

G-3

Beyond the Code

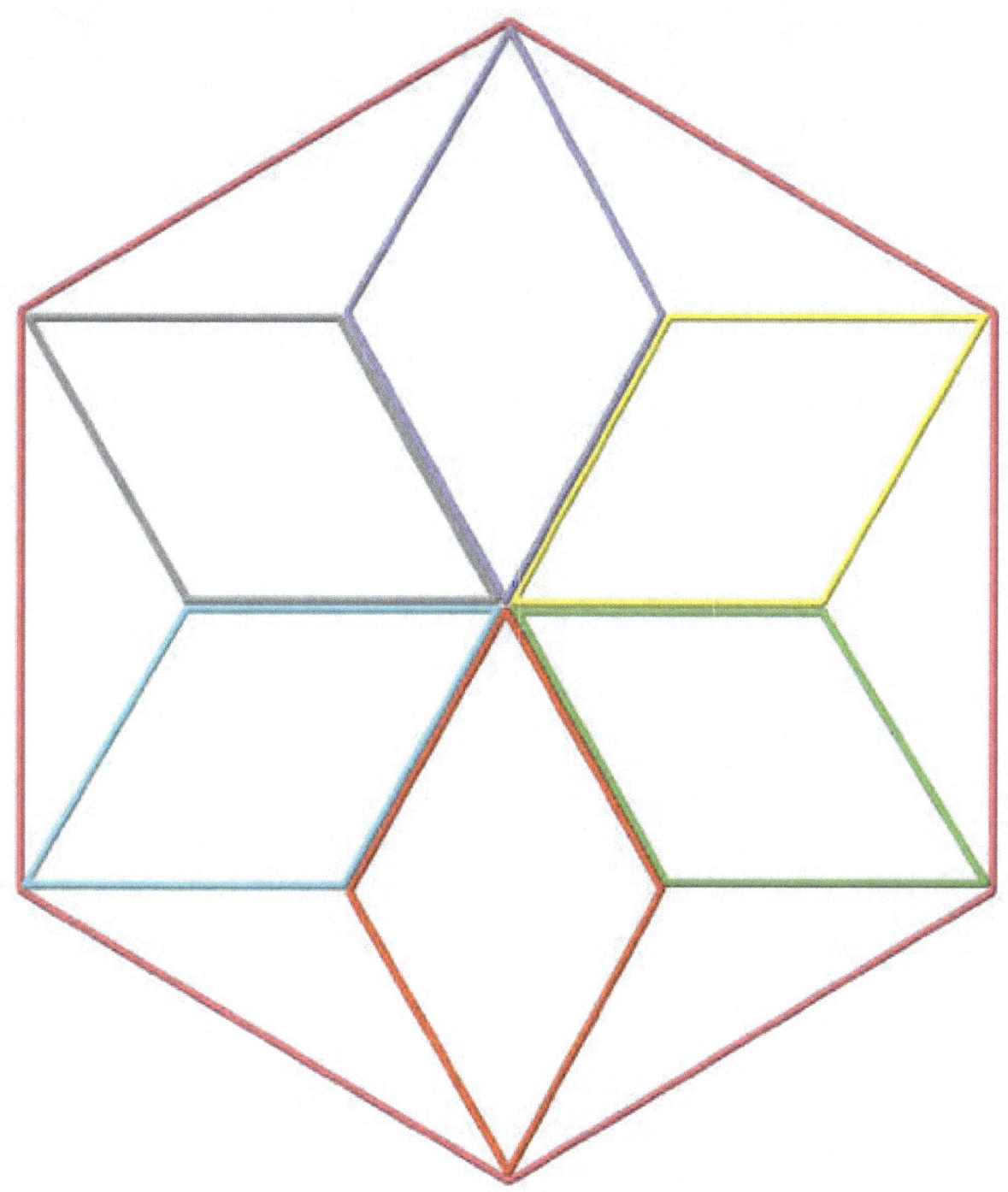

H-1

Beyond the Code

H-2

Reprinted with Permission for noncommercial personal use only. From the Book: Beyond the Code © 2012 Donna Linn

Beyond the Code

H-3

H-4

Reprinted with Permission for noncommercial personal use only. From the Book: Beyond the Code © 2012 Donna Linn

I-1

Reprinted with Permission for noncommercial personal use only. From the Book: Beyond the Code © 2012 Donna Linn

I-2

Beyond the Code

I-3

J-1

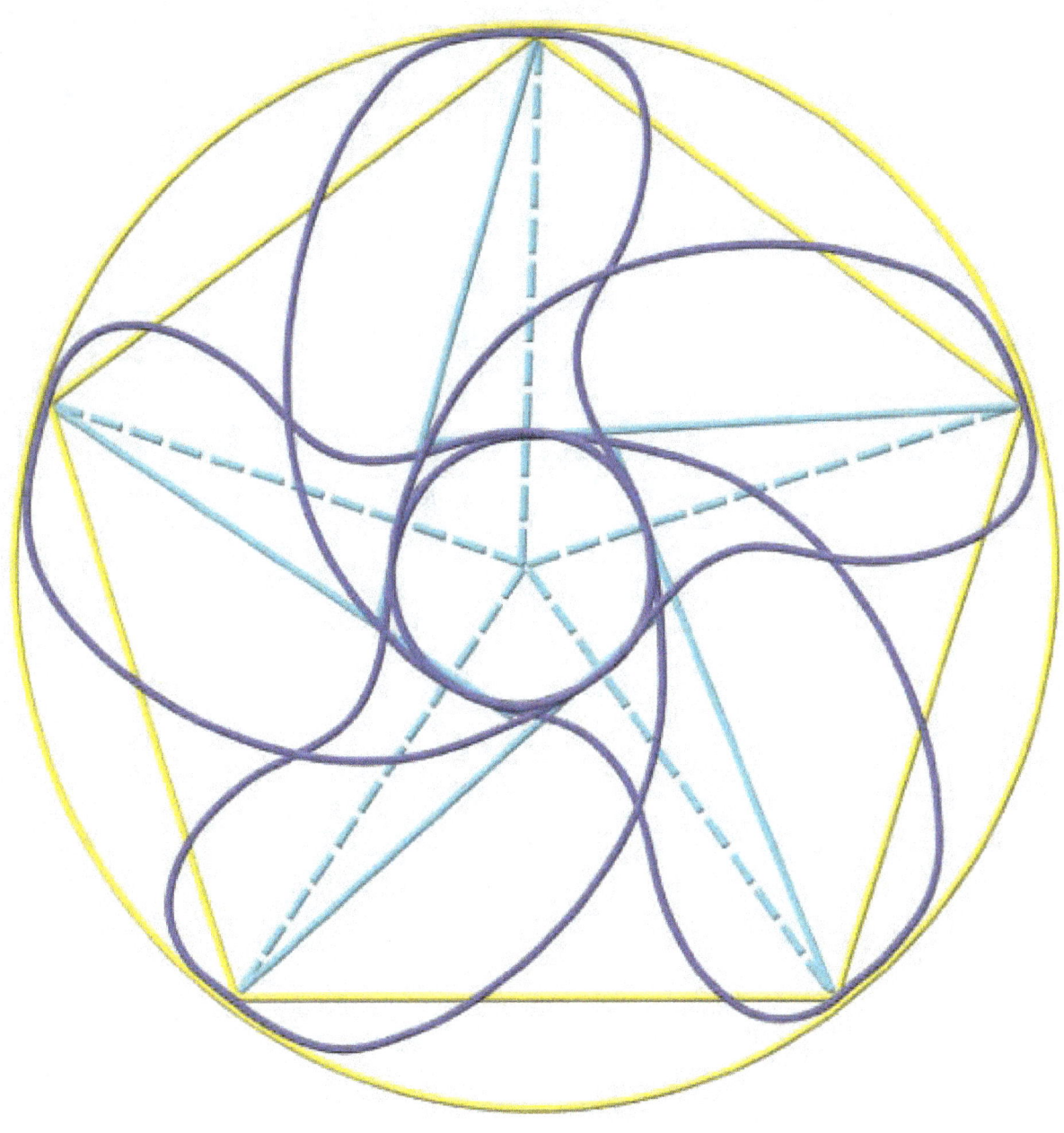

J-2

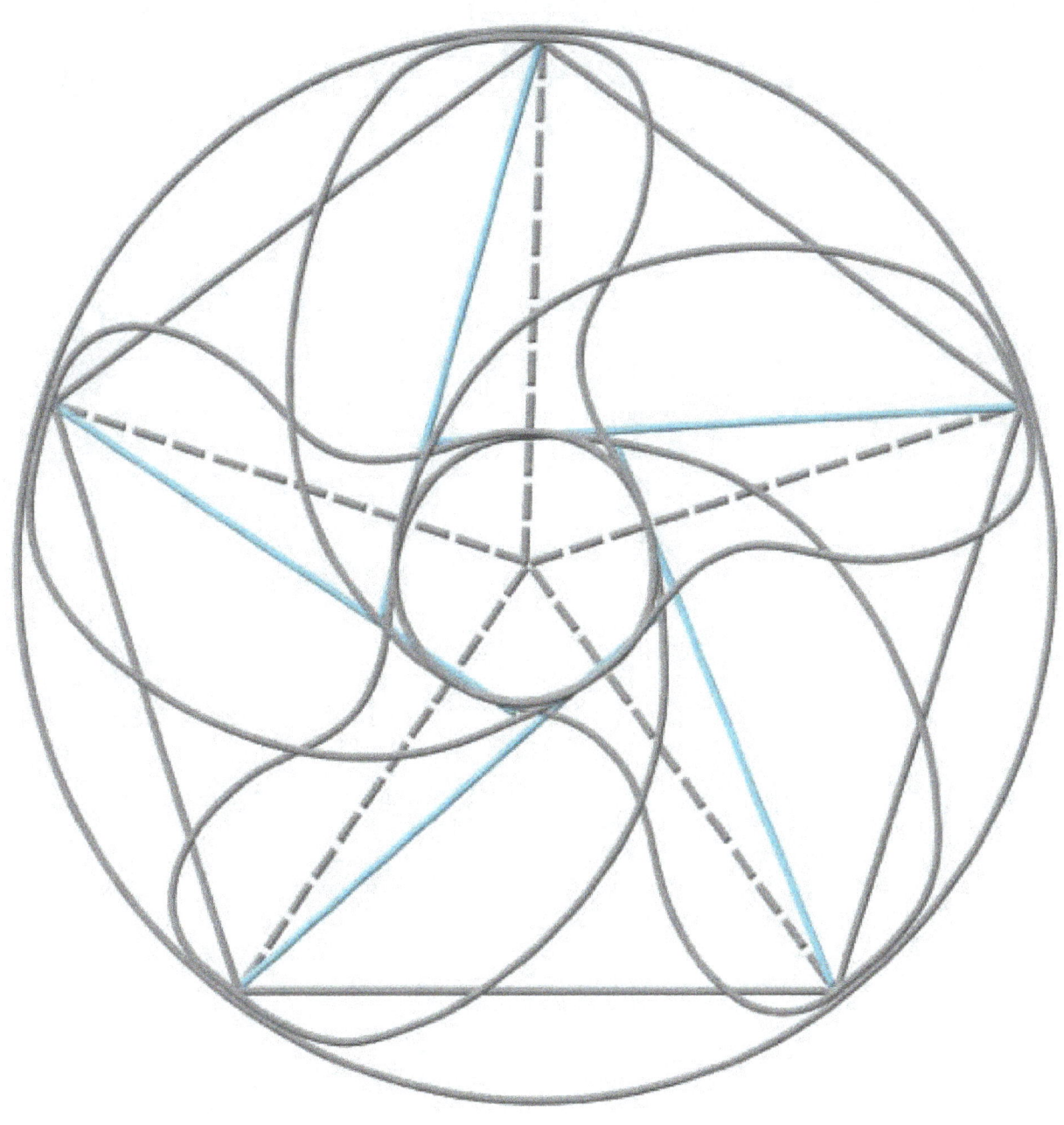

J-3

K-1

Reprinted with Permission for noncommercial personal use only. From the Book: Beyond the Code © 2012 Donna Linn

K-2

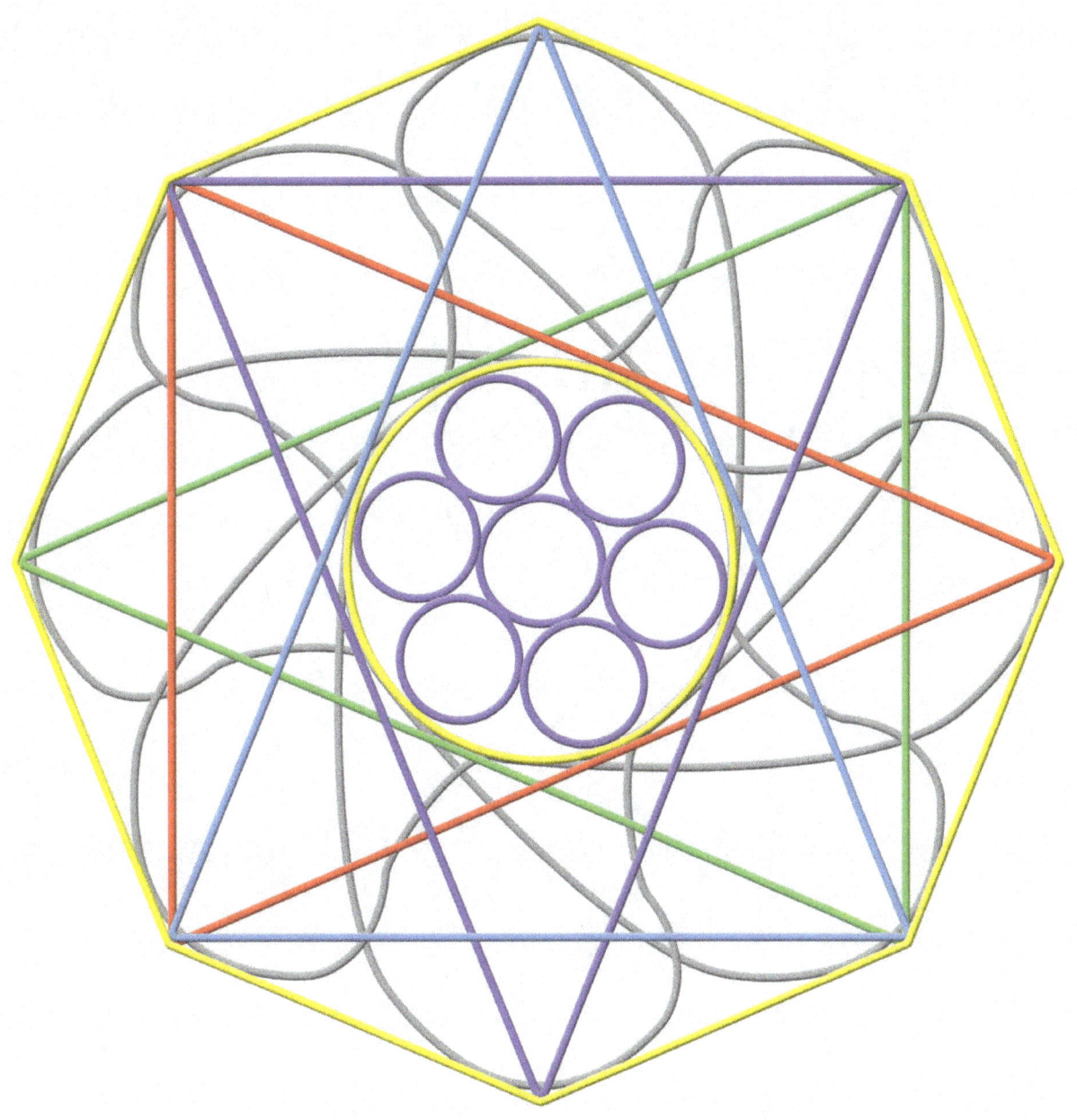

K-3

K-4

Beyond the Code

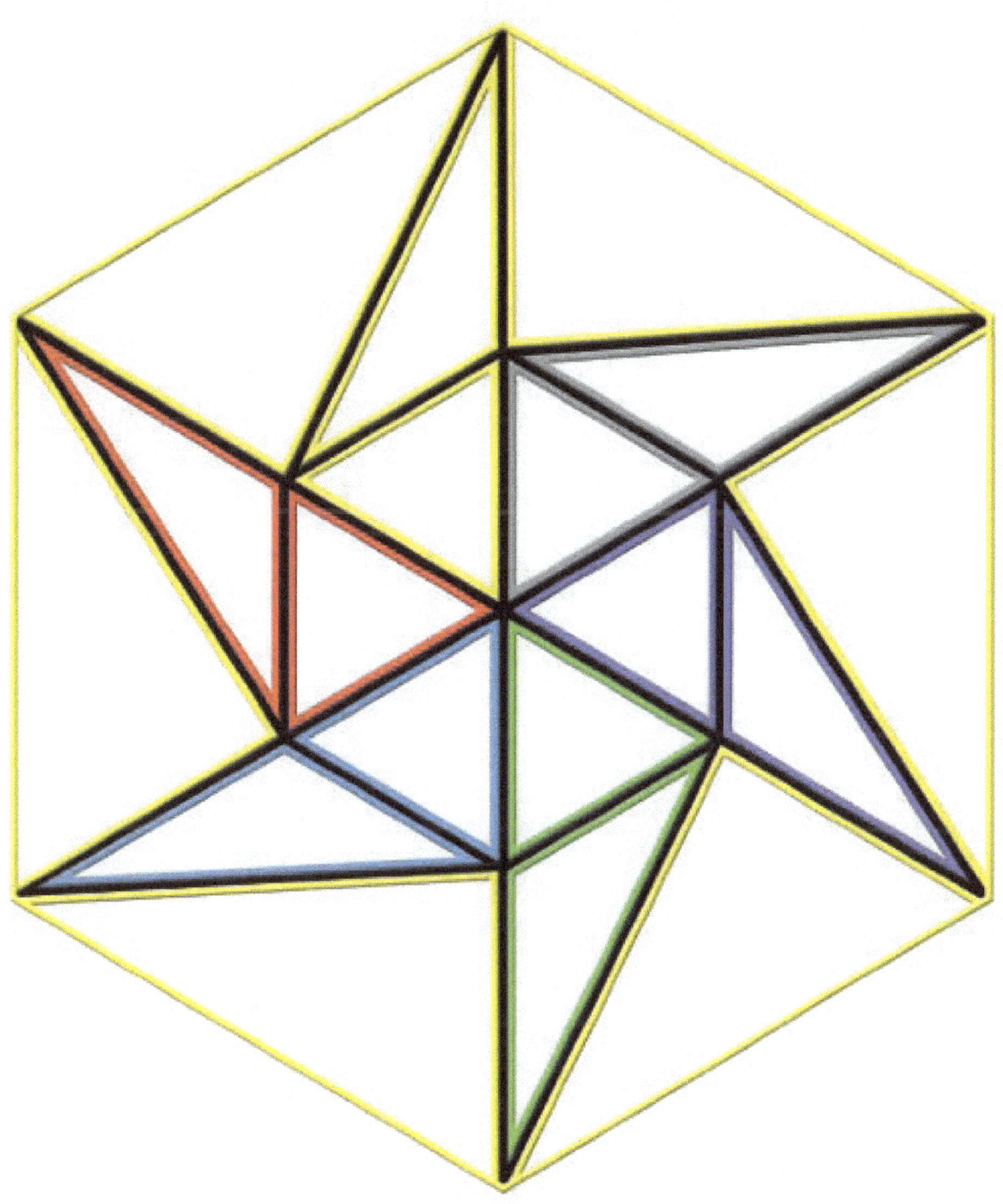

L-1

Beyond the Code

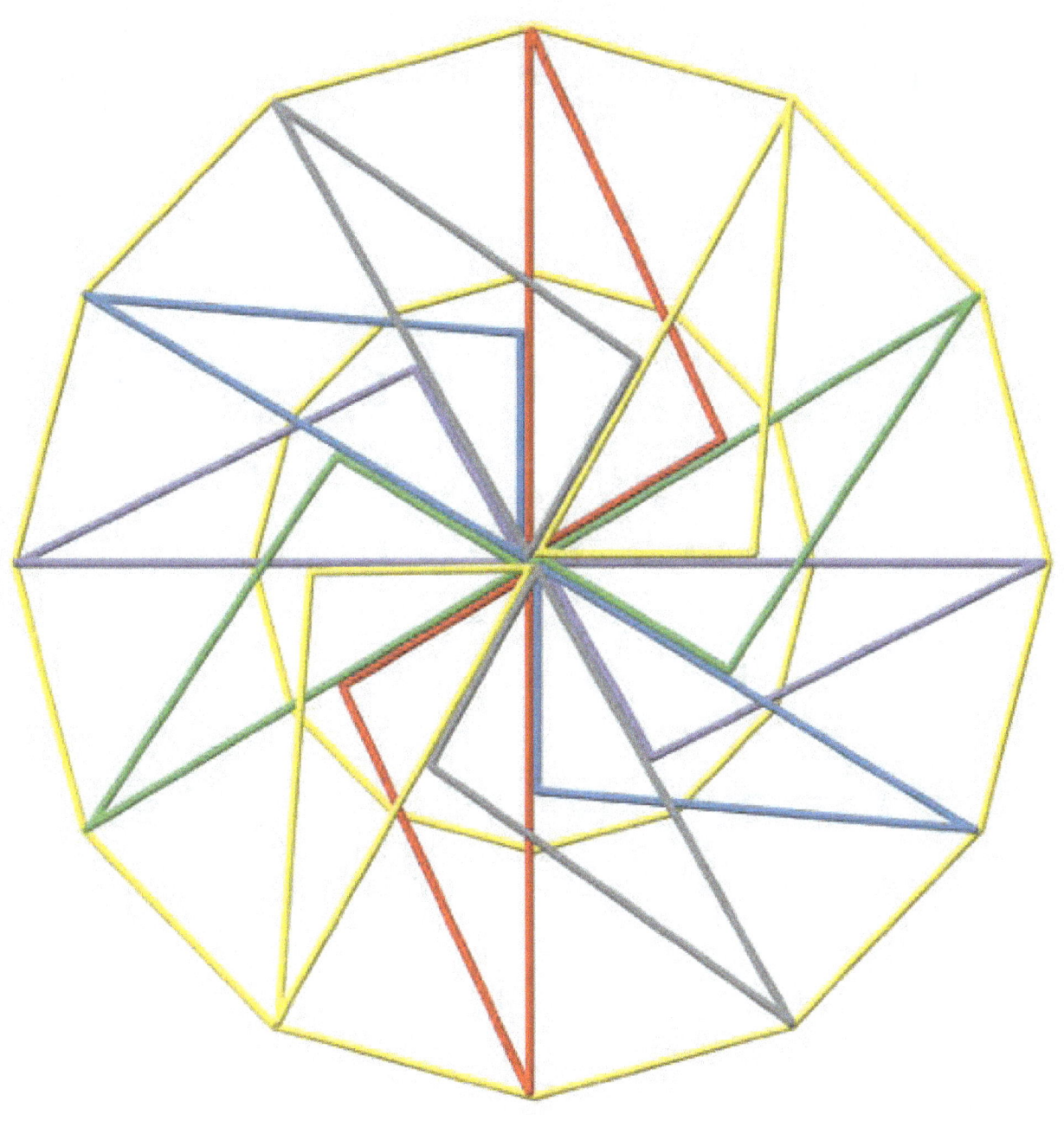

L-2

Beyond the Code

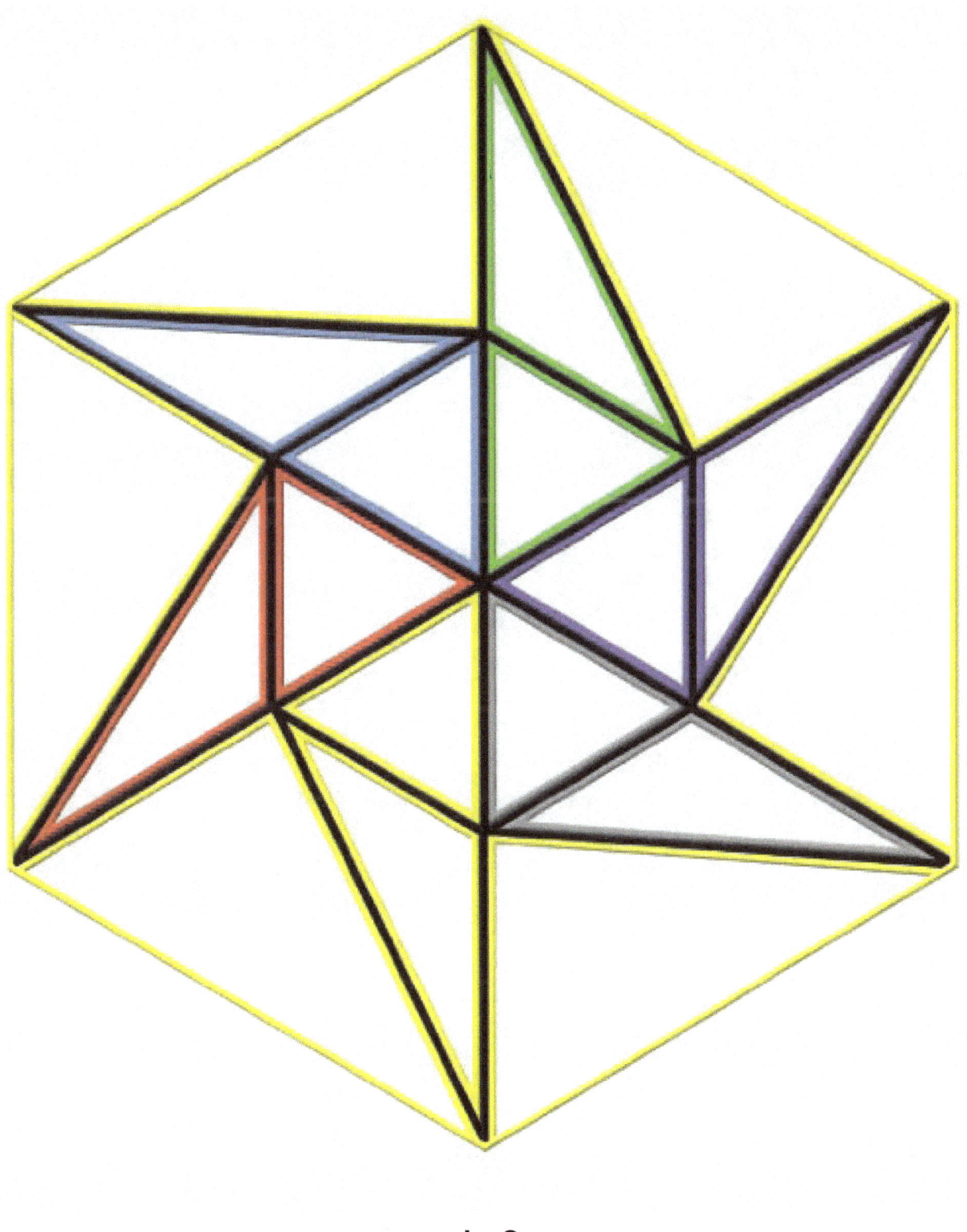

L-3

M-1

Reprinted with Permission for noncommercial personal use only. From the Book: Beyond the Code © 2012 Donna Linn

M-2

Beyond the Code

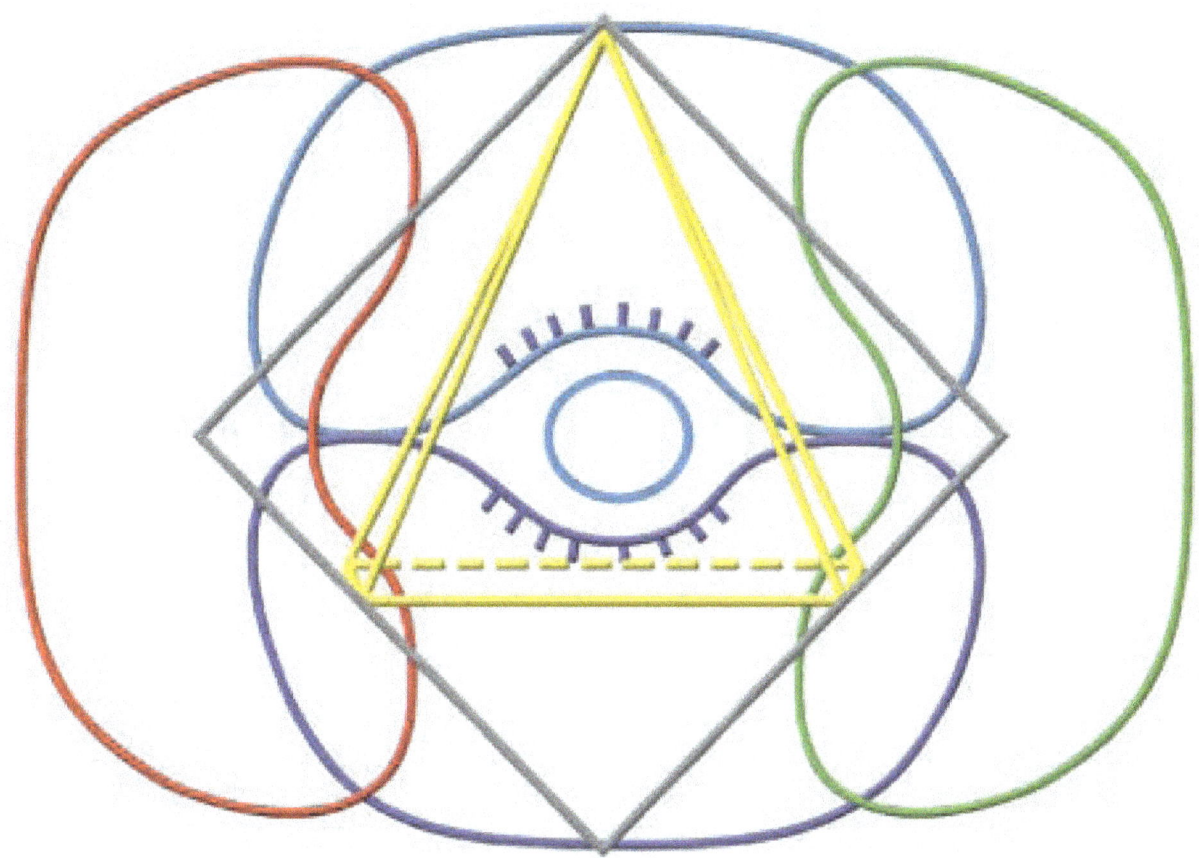

M-3

M-4

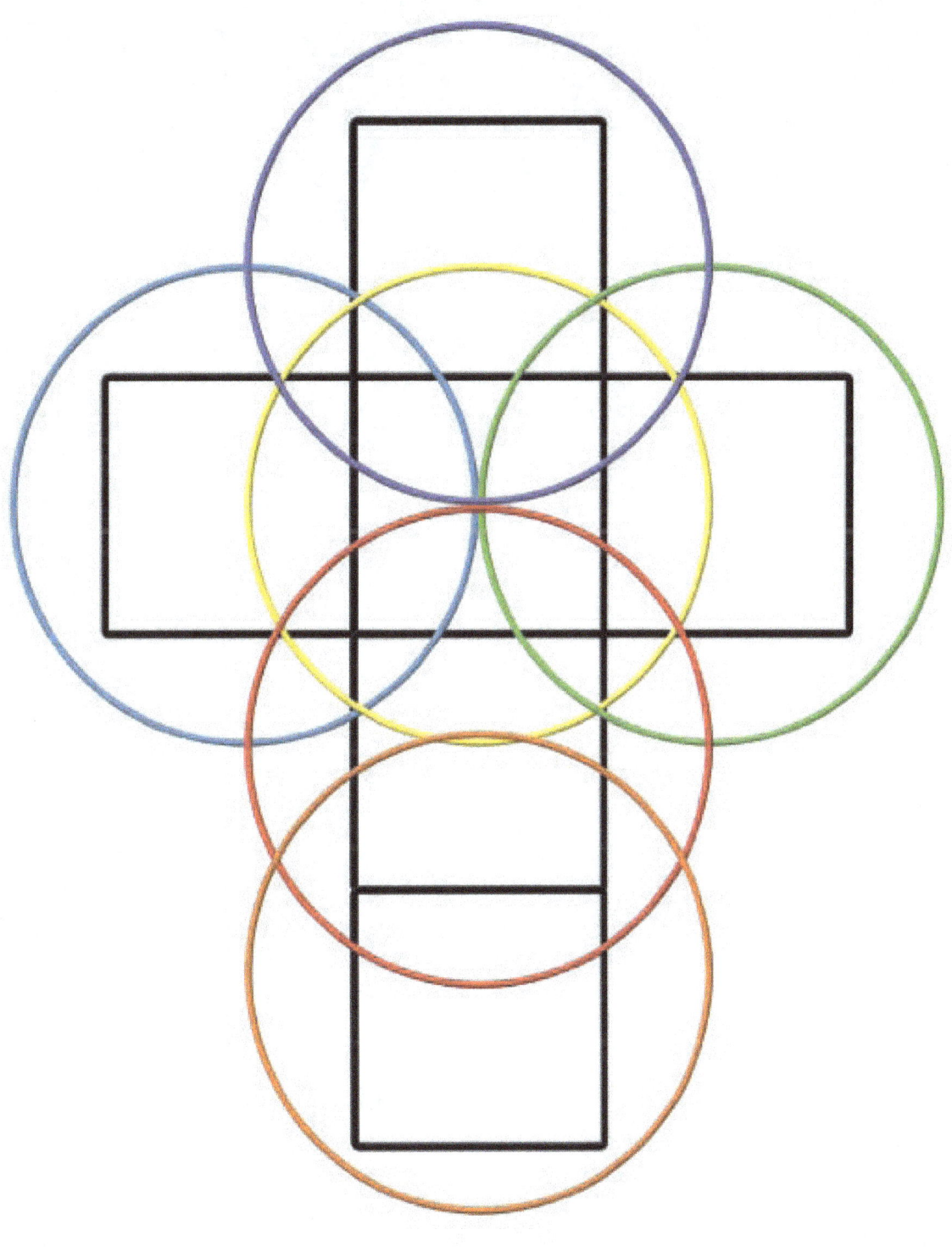

N-1

N-2

Beyond the Code

N-3

Reprinted with Permission for noncommercial personal use only. From the Book: Beyond the Code © 2012 Donna Linn

Beyond the Code

O-1

O-2

0-3

P-1

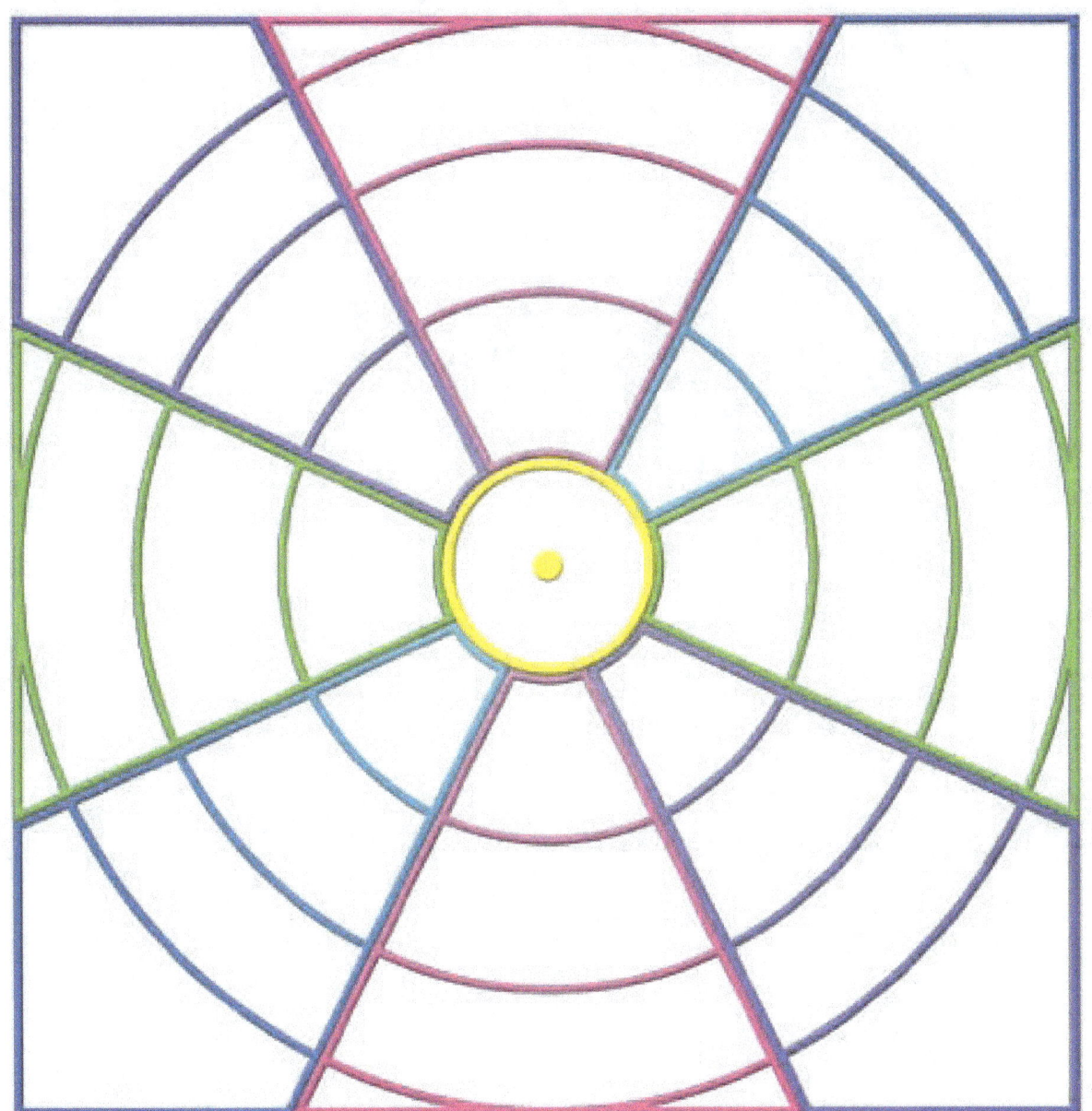

P-2

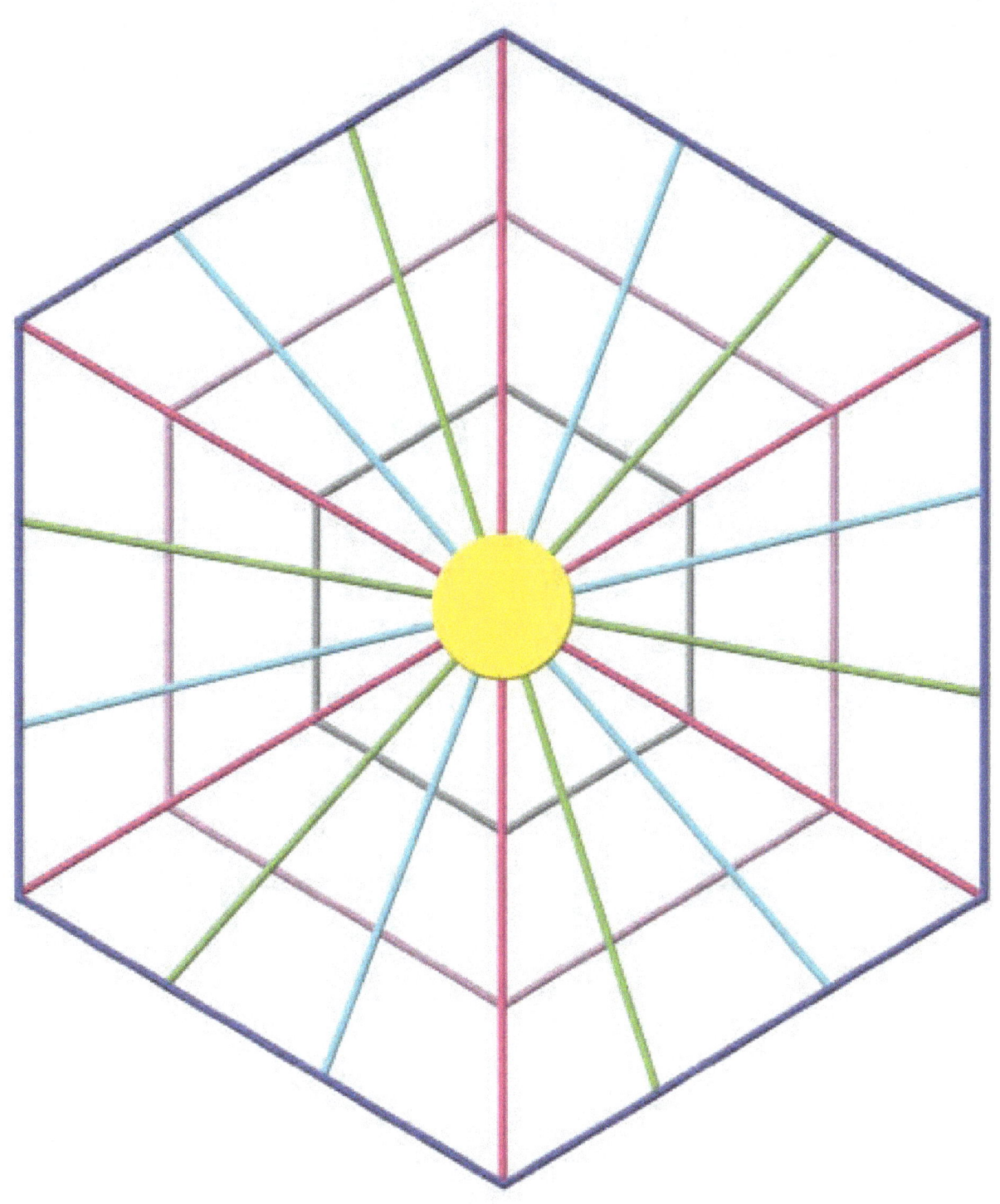

P-3

Beyond the Code

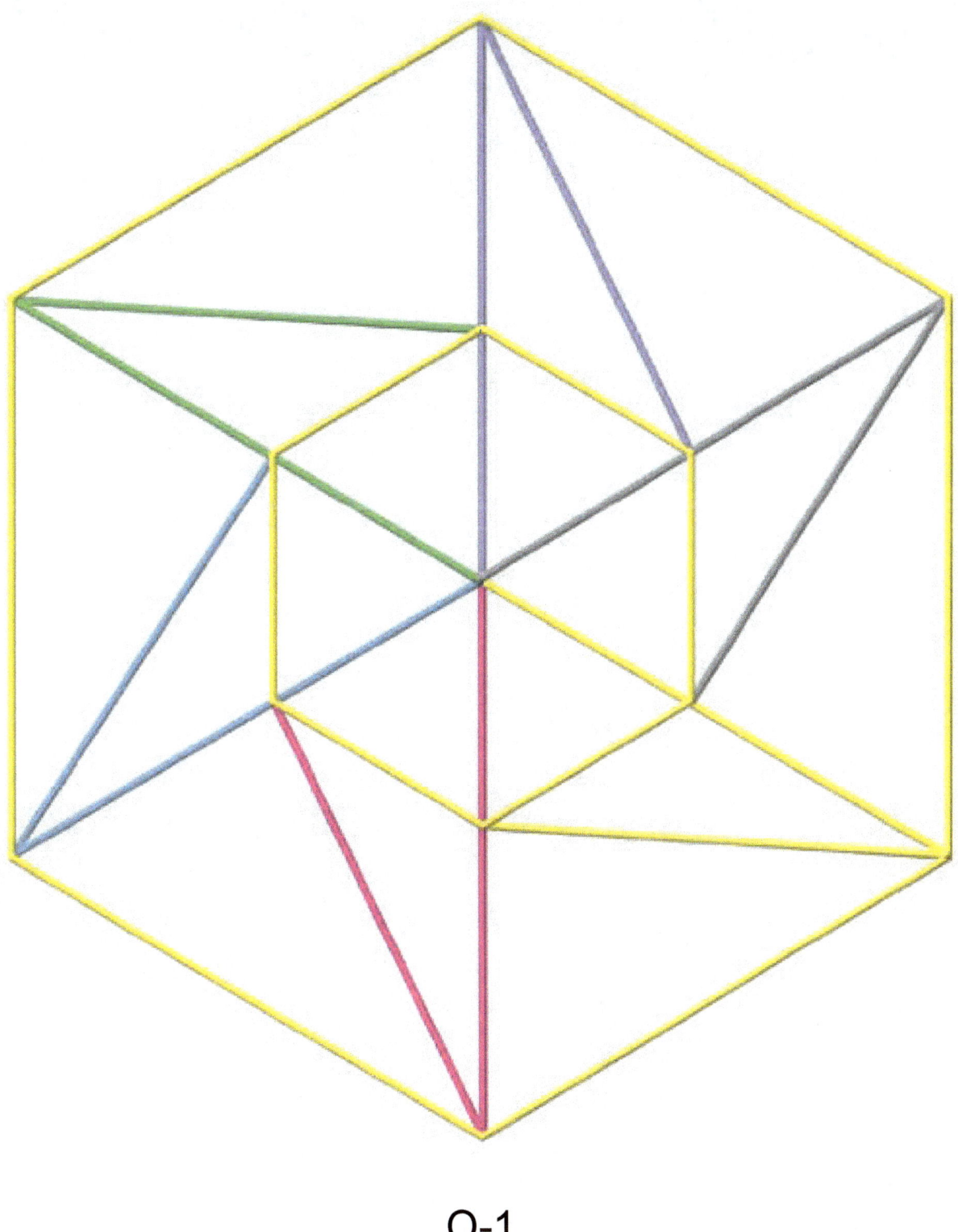

Q-1

Beyond the Code

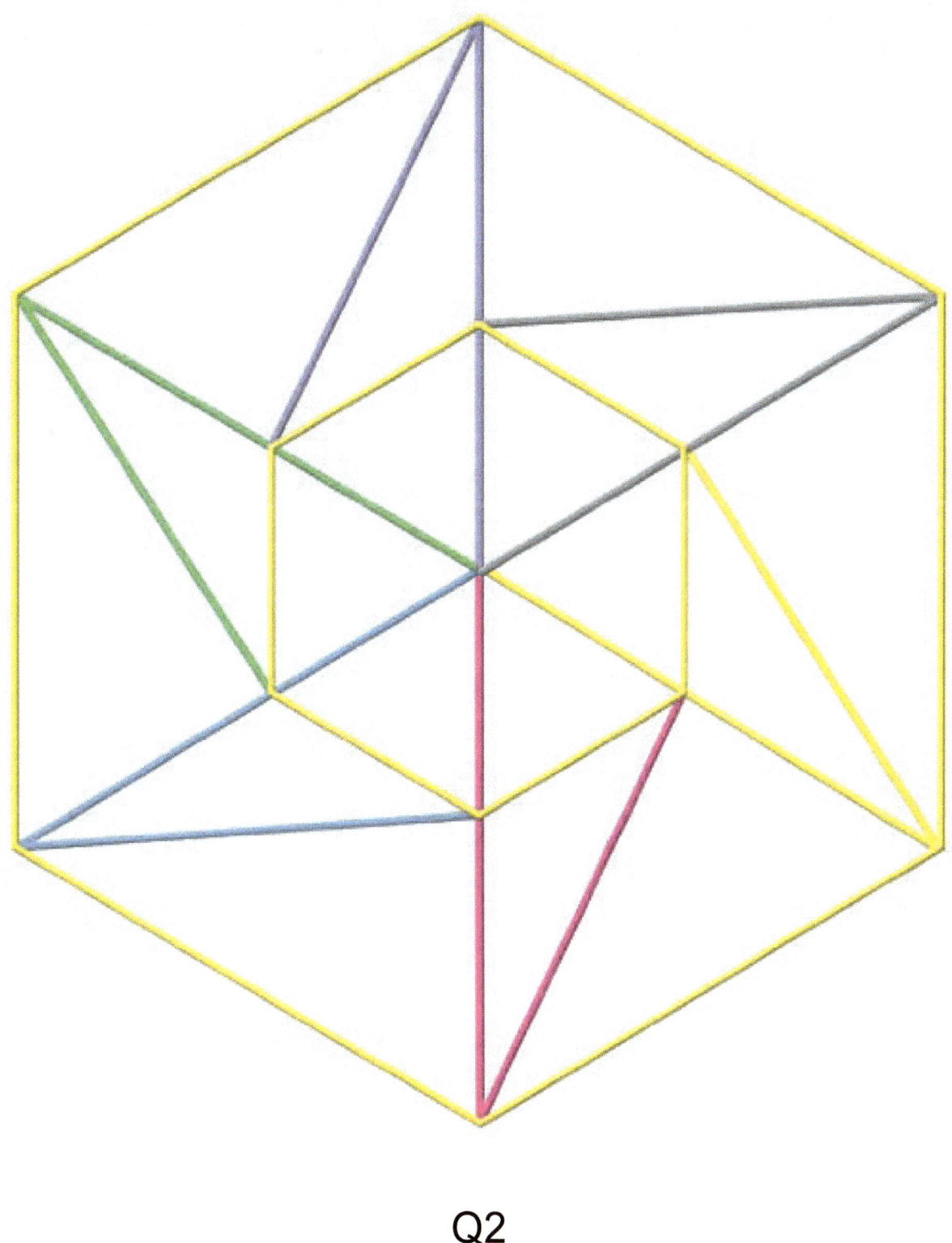

Q2

R-1

R-2

Beyond the Code

R-3

Reprinted with Permission for noncommercial personal use only. From the Book: Beyond the Code © 2012 Donna Linn

Beyond the Code

S-1

Beyond the Code

S-2

Beyond the Code

S-3

Reprinted with Permission for noncommercial personal use only. From the Book: Beyond the Code © 2012 Donna Linn

Beyond the Code

T-1

Beyond the Code

T-2

T-3

Beyond the Code

T-4

Beyond the Code

U-1

Beyond the Code

U-2

U-3

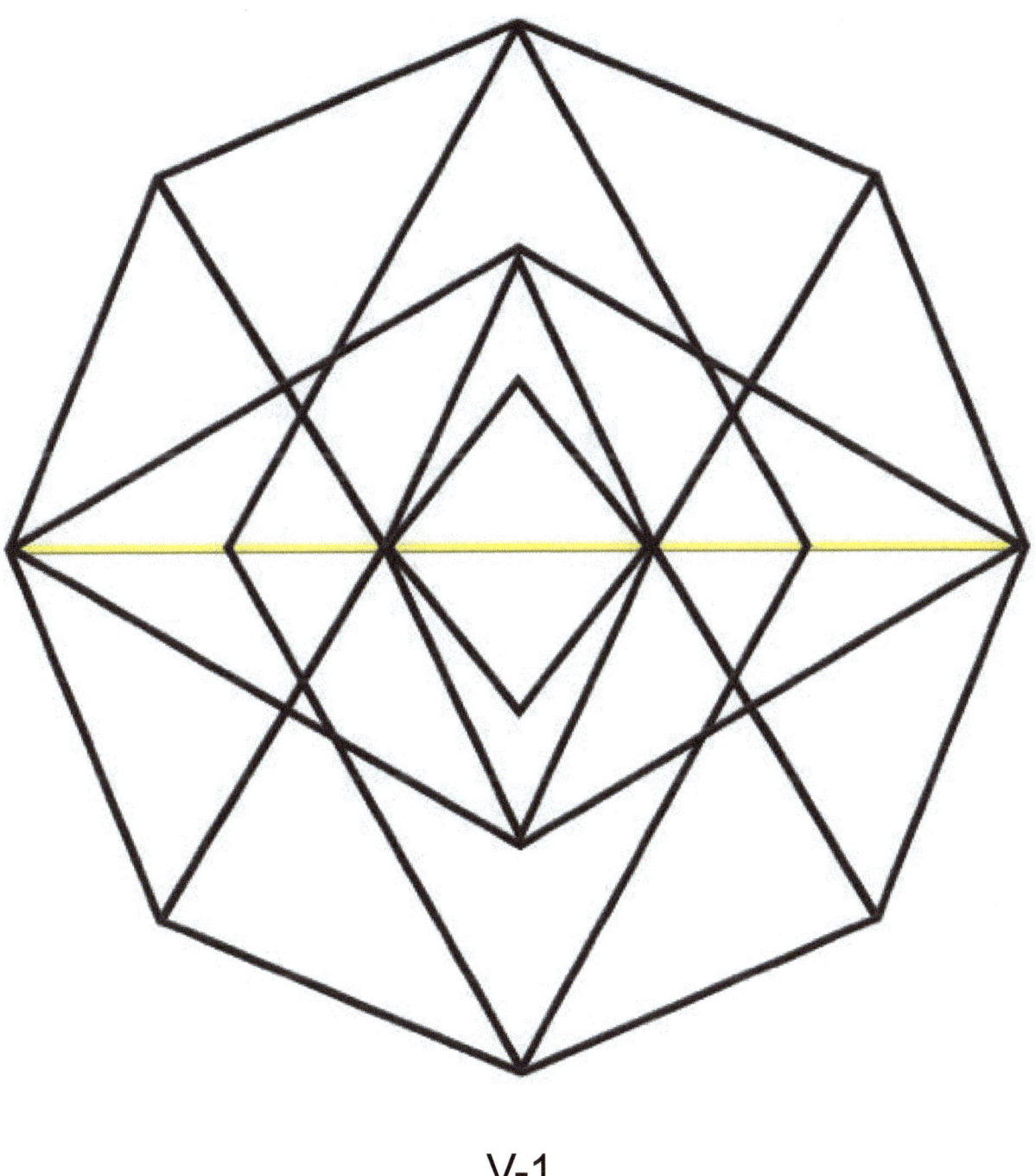

V-1

Reprinted with Permission for noncommercial personal use only. From the Book: Beyond the Code © 2012 Donna Linn

Beyond the Code

V-2

Beyond the Code

V-3

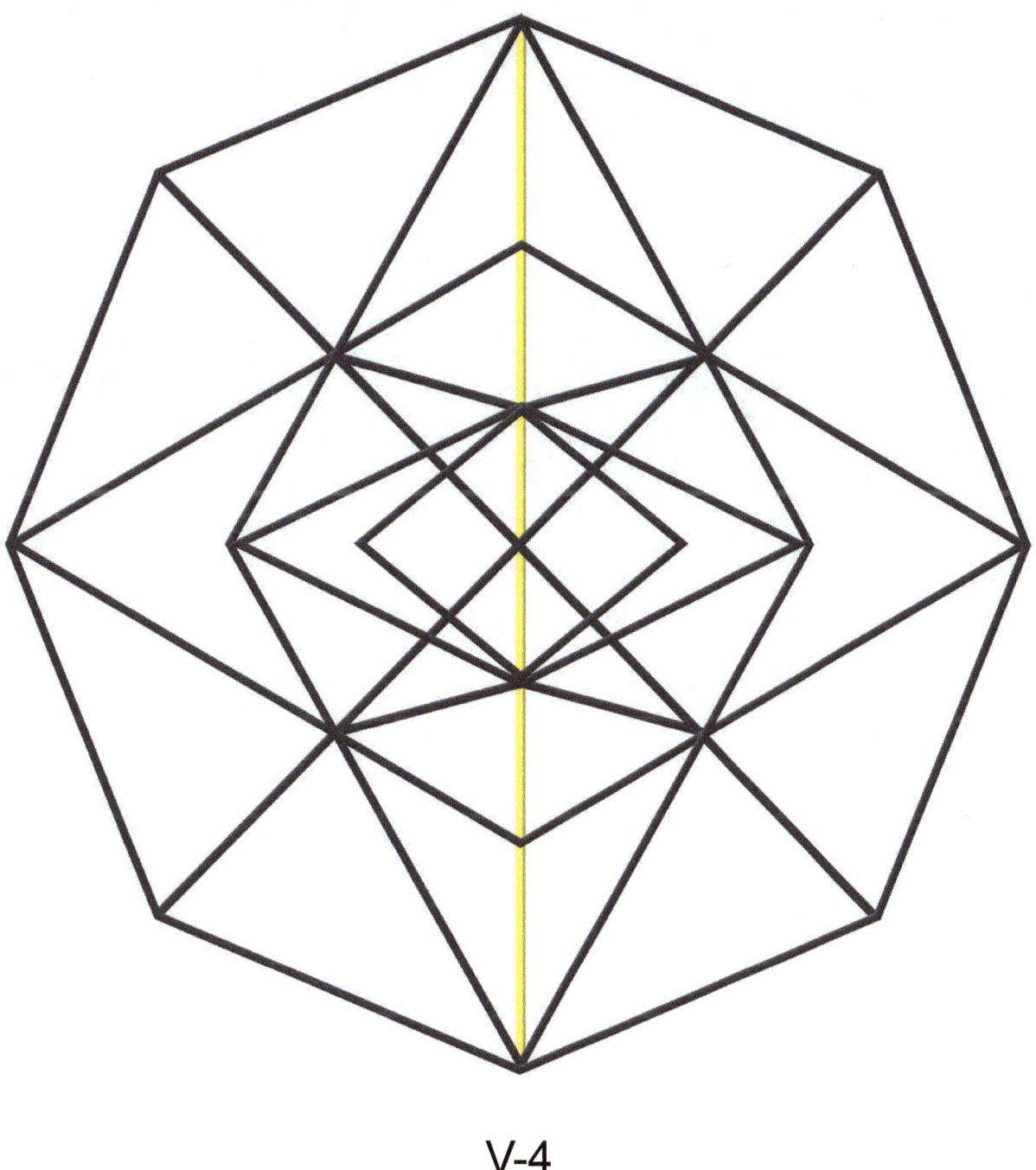

V-4

Beyond the Code

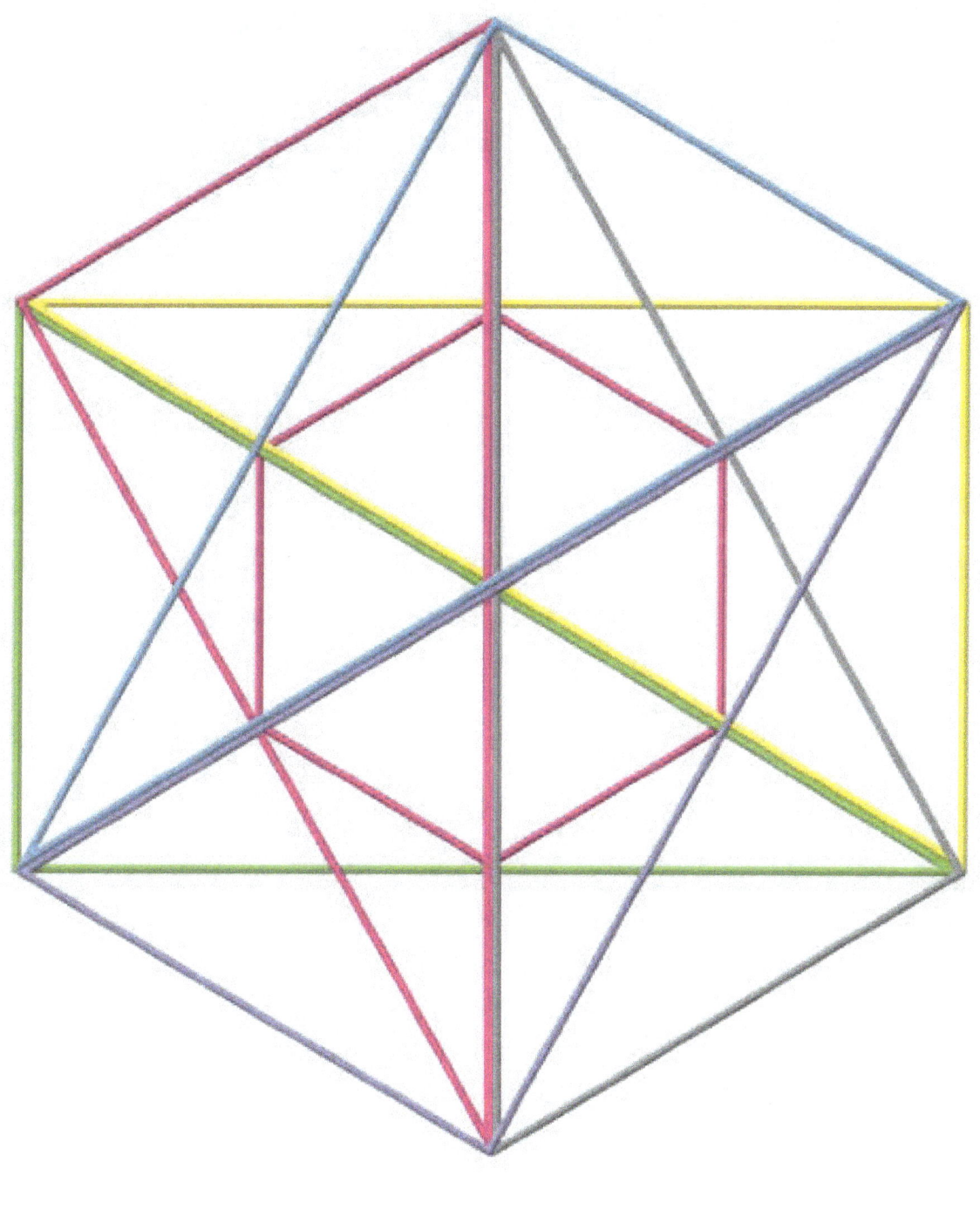

V-5

W-1

Beyond the Code

W-2

W-3

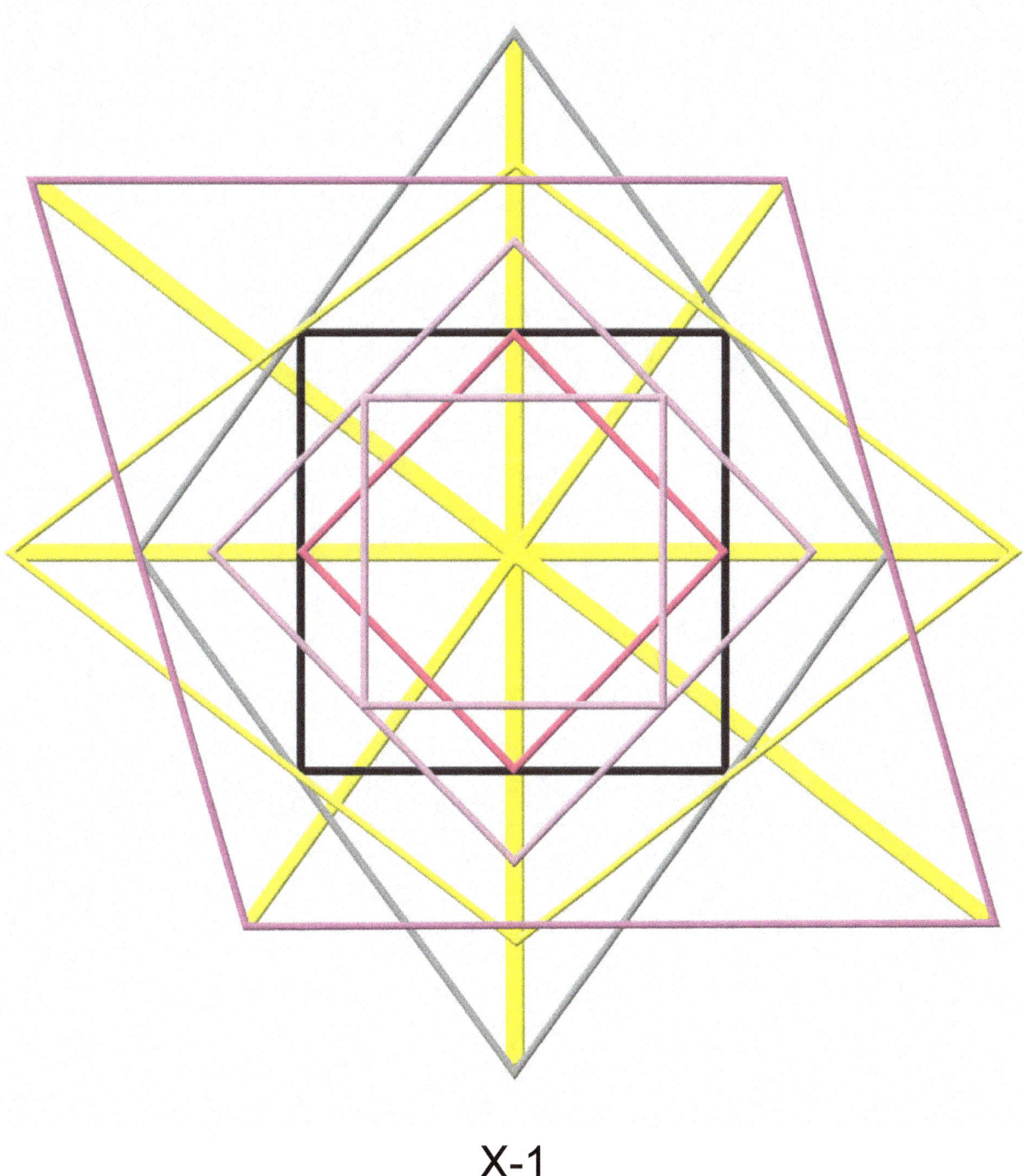

X-1

X-2

Beyond the Code

X-3

Beyond the Code

Y-1

Reprinted with Permission for noncommercial personal use only. From the Book: Beyond the Code © 2012 Donna Linn

Y-2

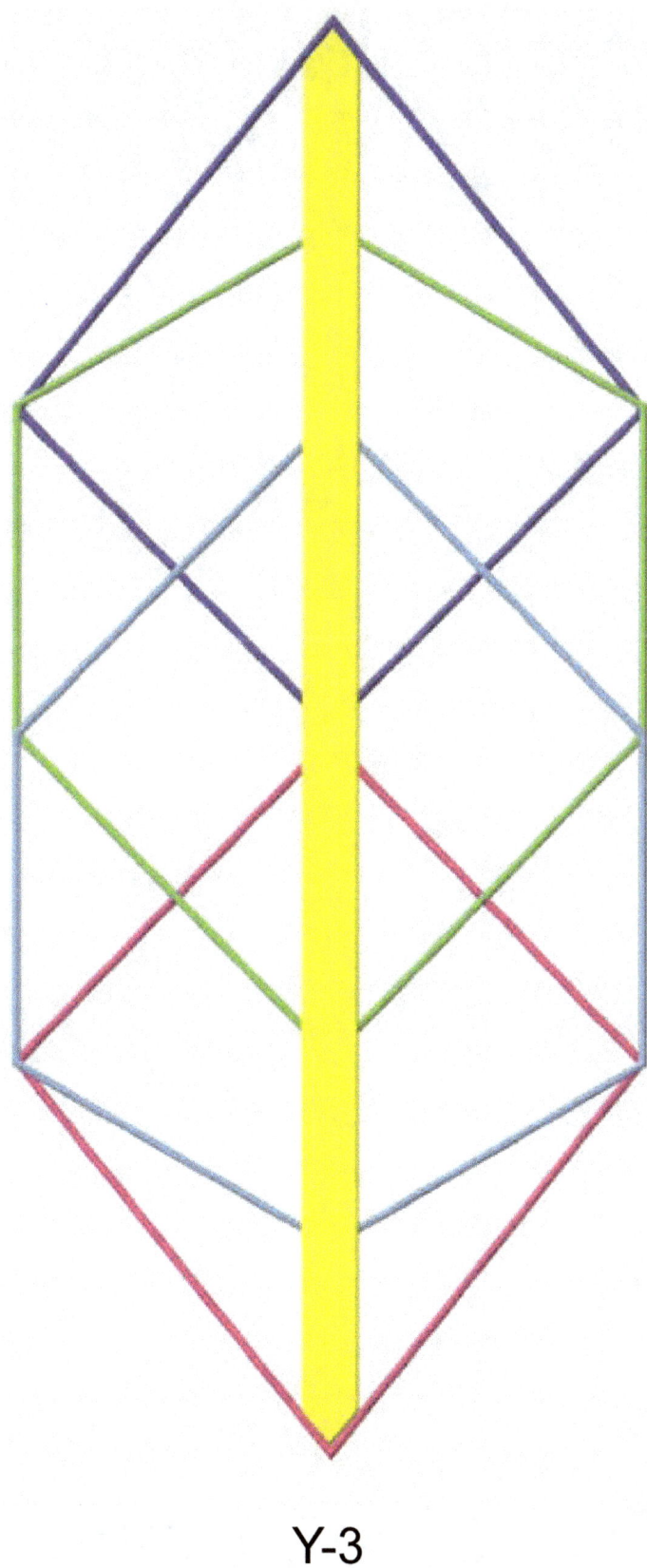

Y-3

Beyond the Code

Y-4

Beyond the Code

Y-5

Beyond the Code

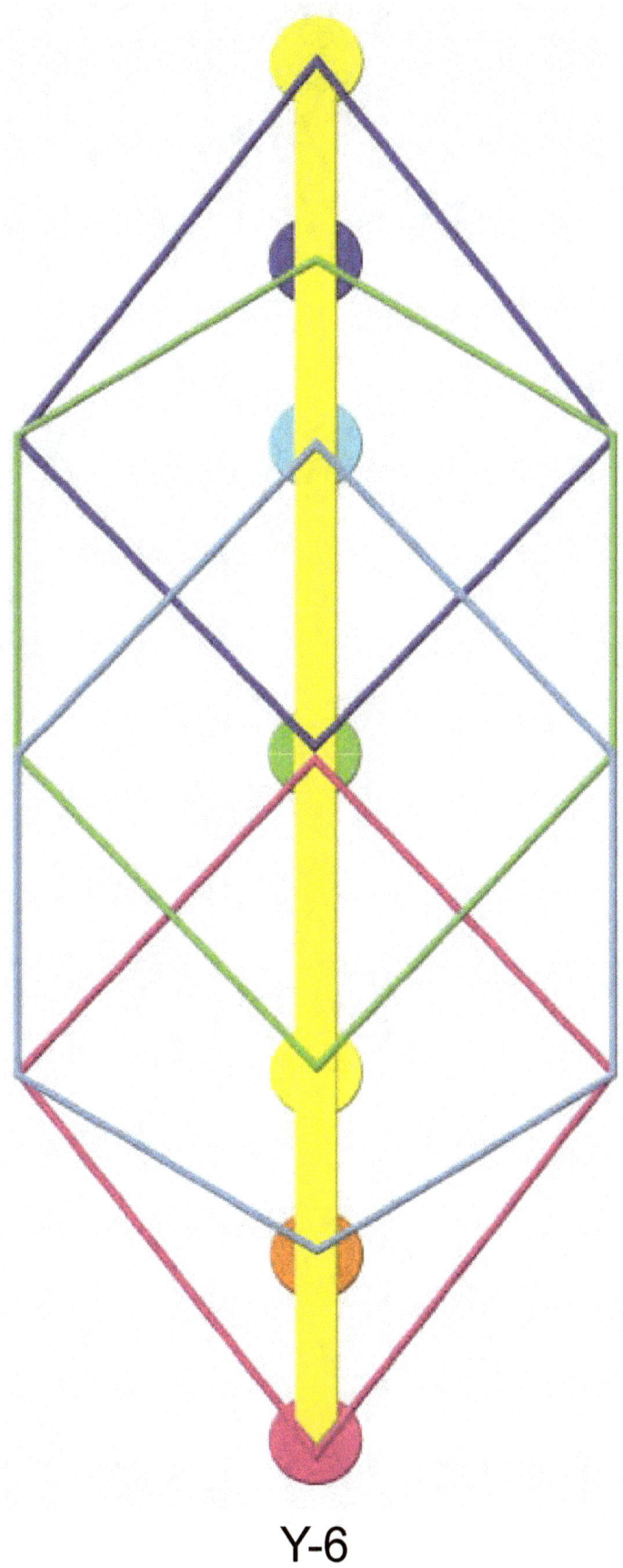

Y-6

Beyond the Code

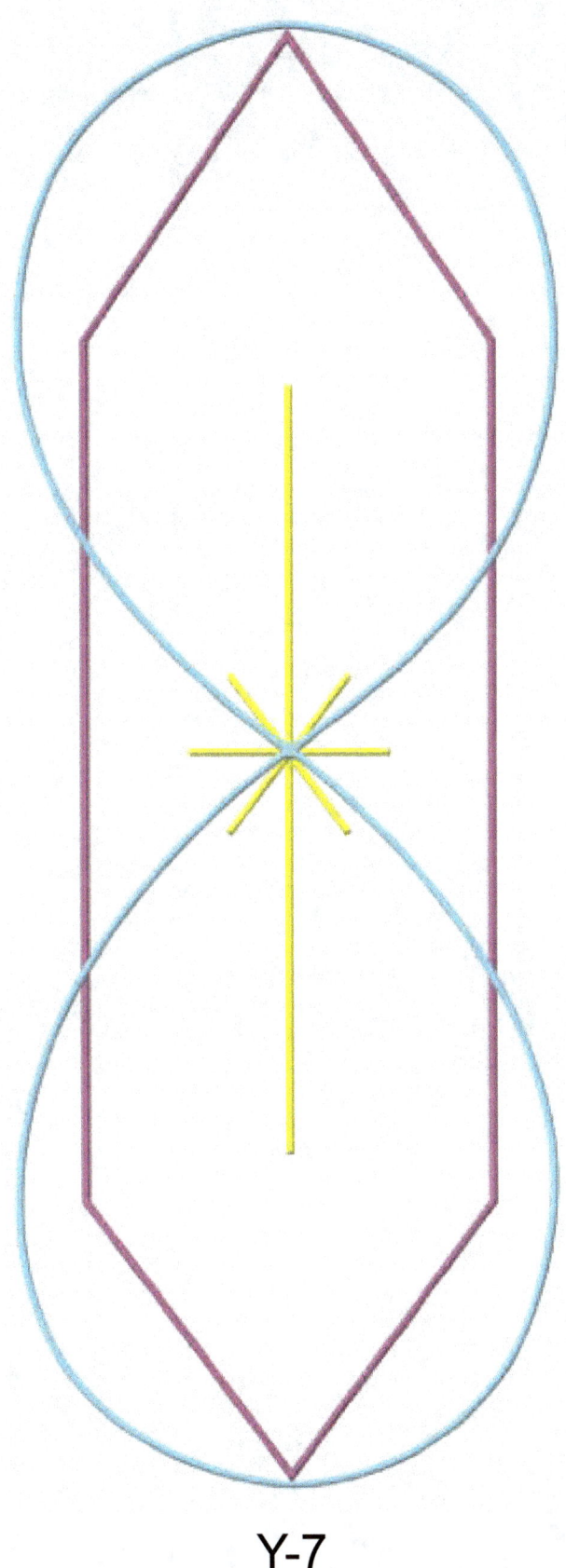

Y-7

Z-1

Beyond the Code

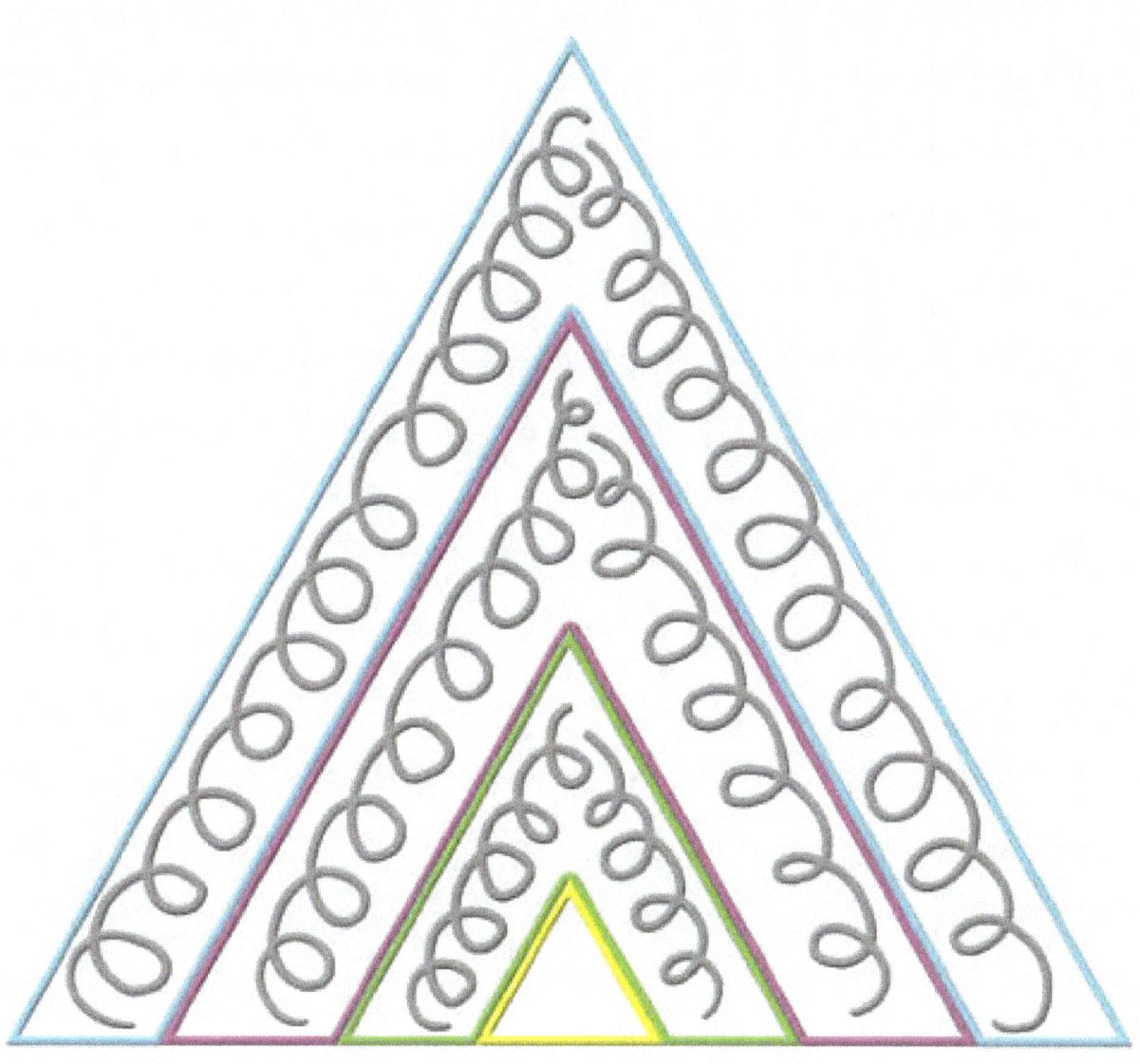

Z-2

Beyond the Code

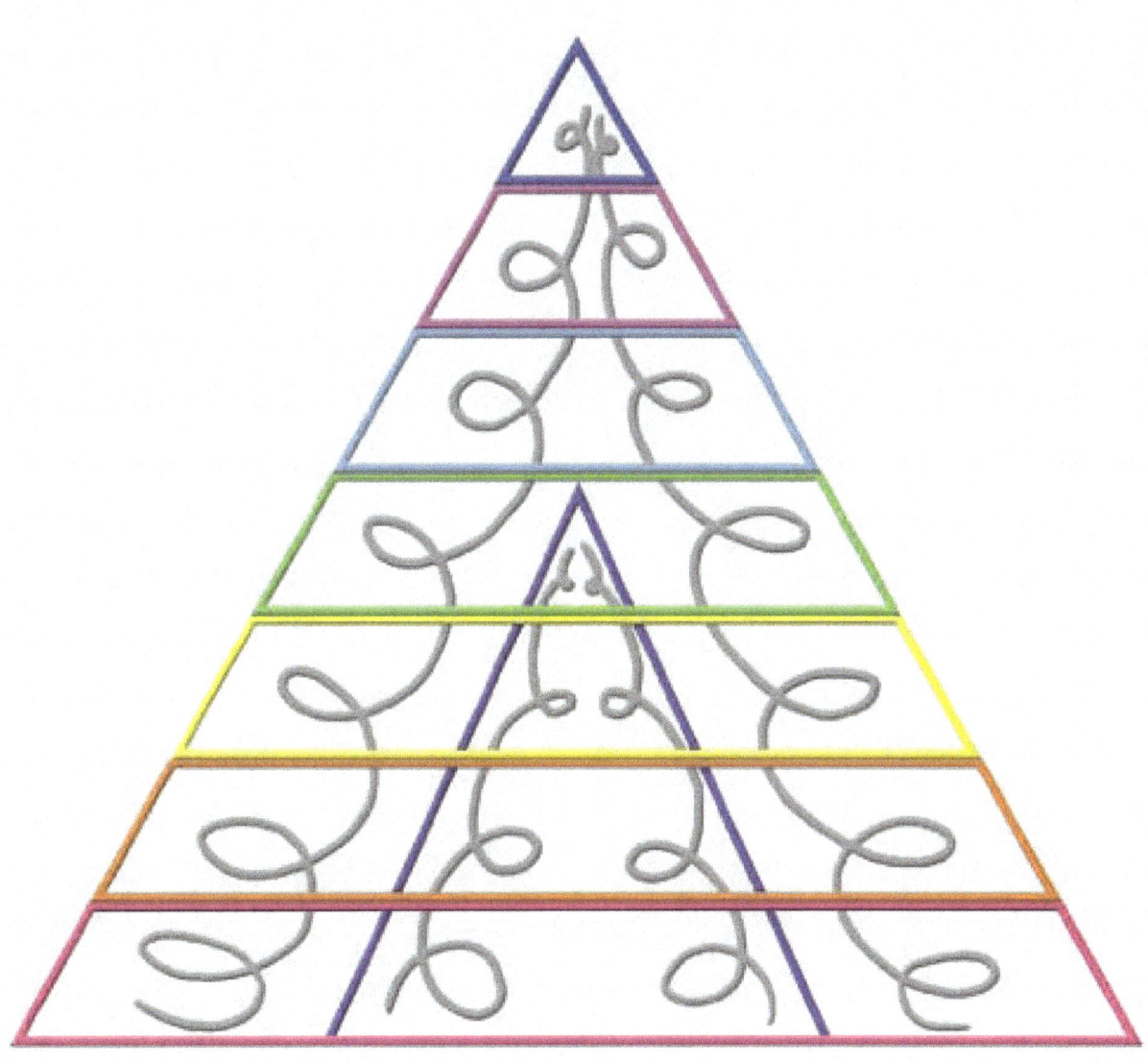

Z-3

Z-4

Beyond the Code

AA-1

Reprinted with Permission for noncommercial personal use only. From the Book: Beyond the Code © 2012 Donna Linn

Beyond the Code

AA-2

Beyond the Code

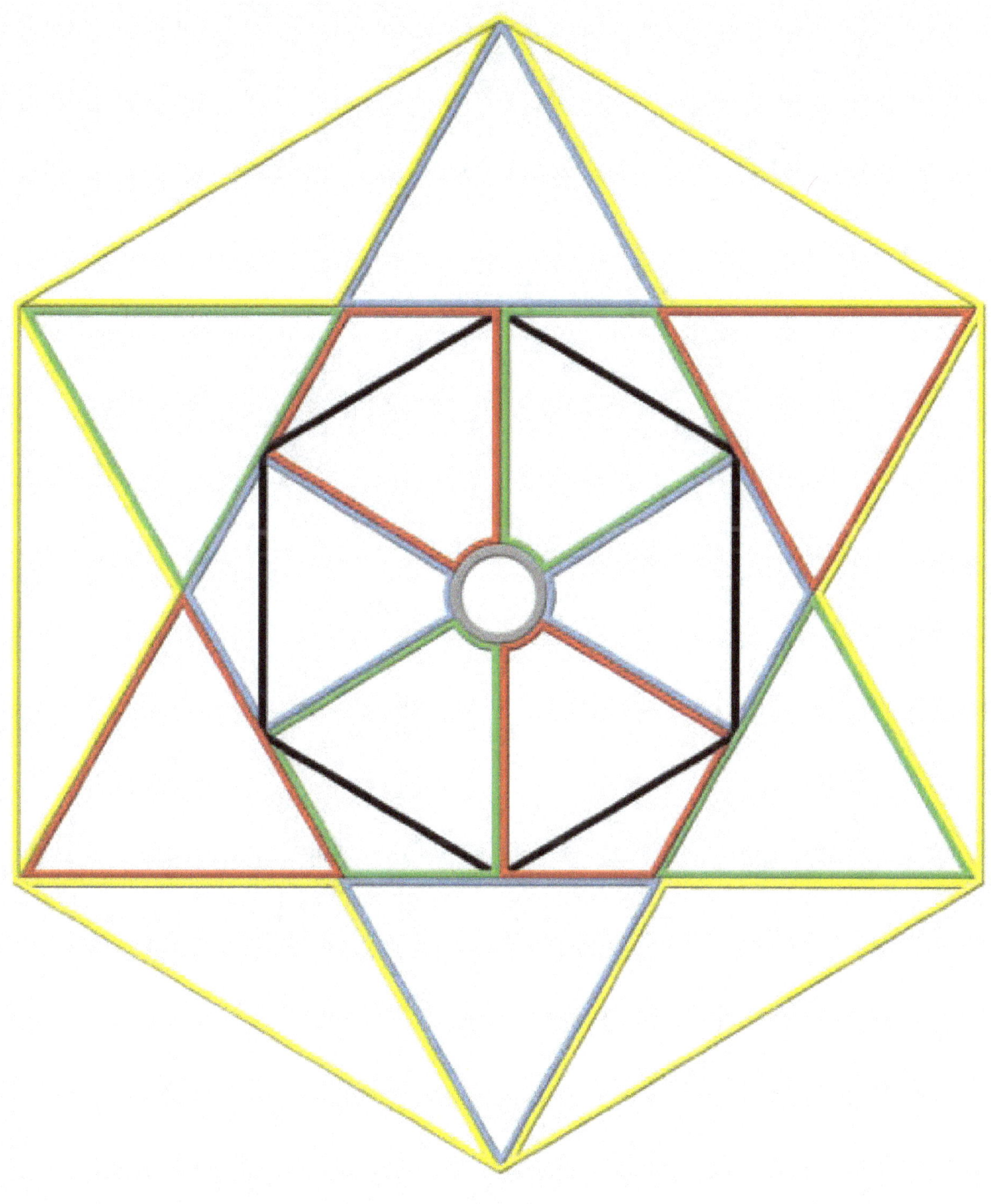

AA-3

Reprinted with Permission for noncommercial personal use only. From the Book: Beyond the Code © 2012 Donna Linn

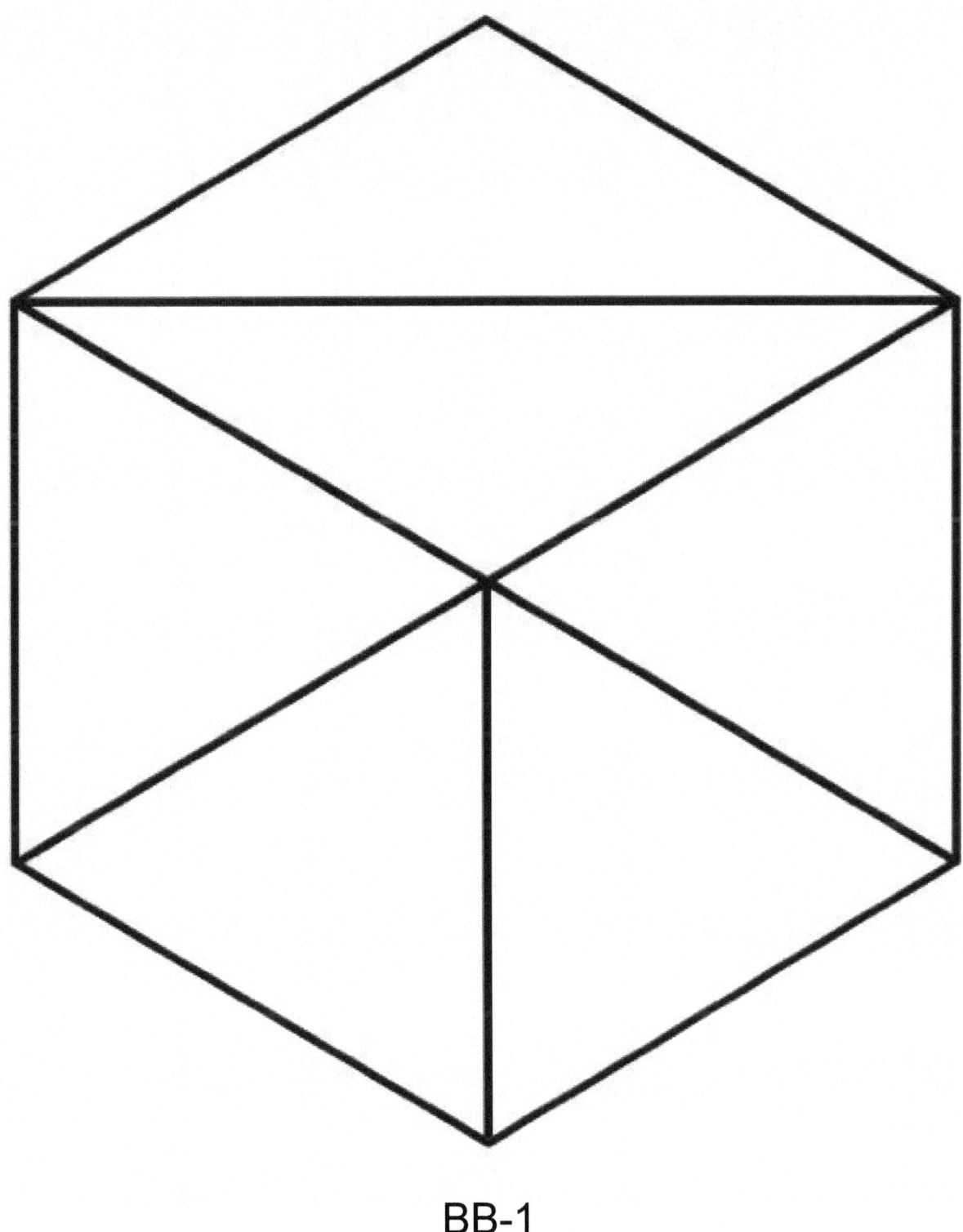

BB-1

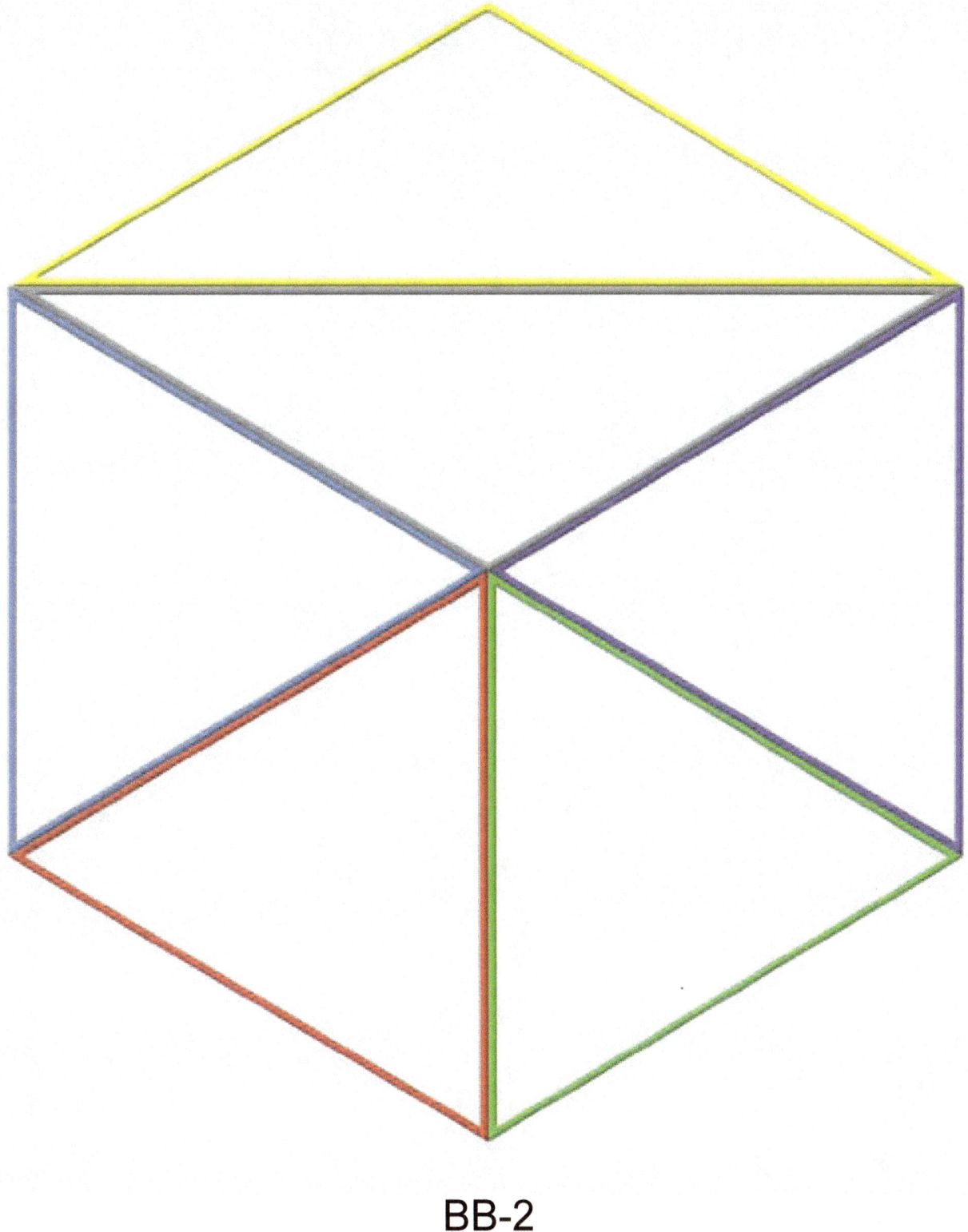

BB-2

Beyond the Code

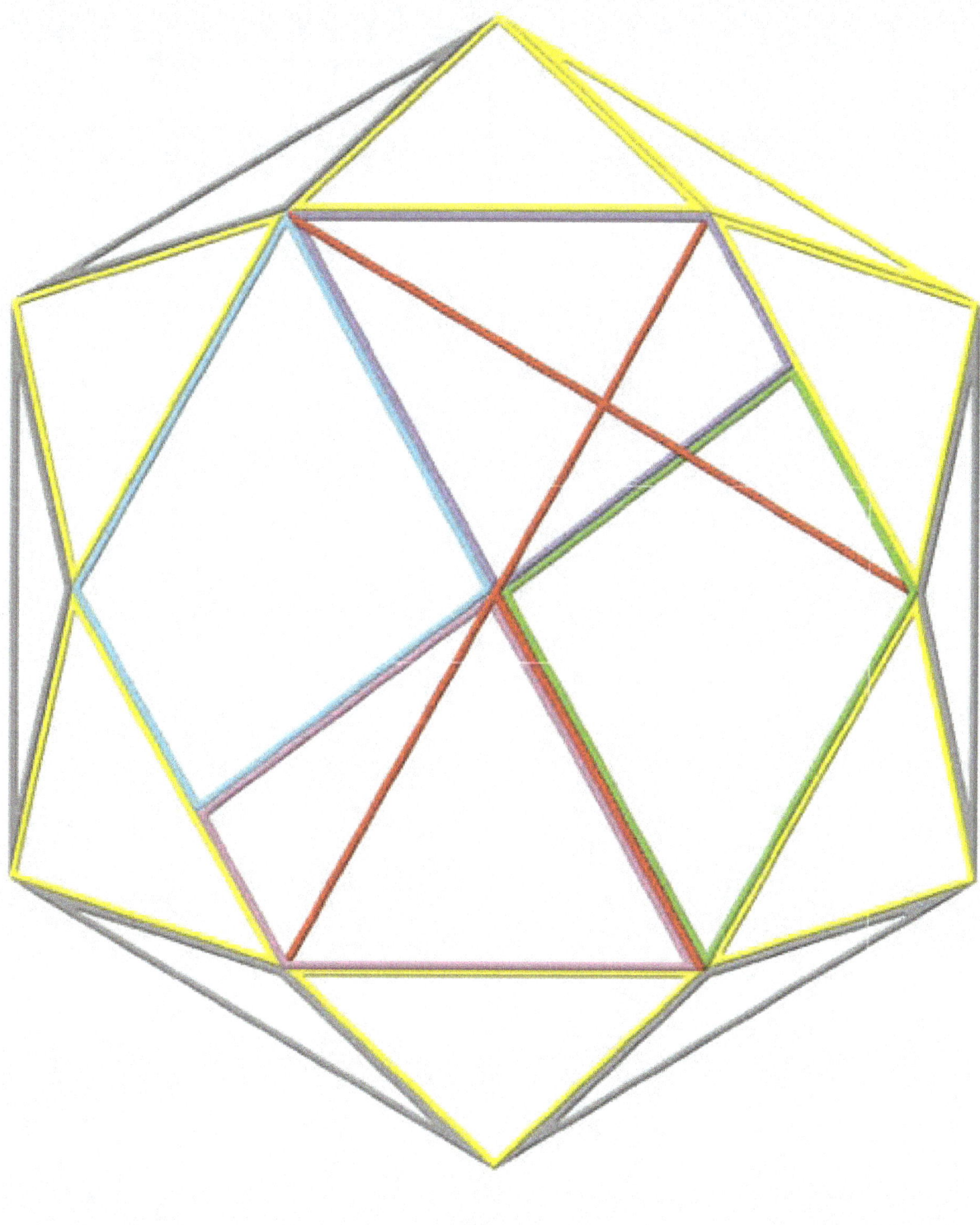

BB-3

CC-1

Beyond the Code

CC-2

CC-3

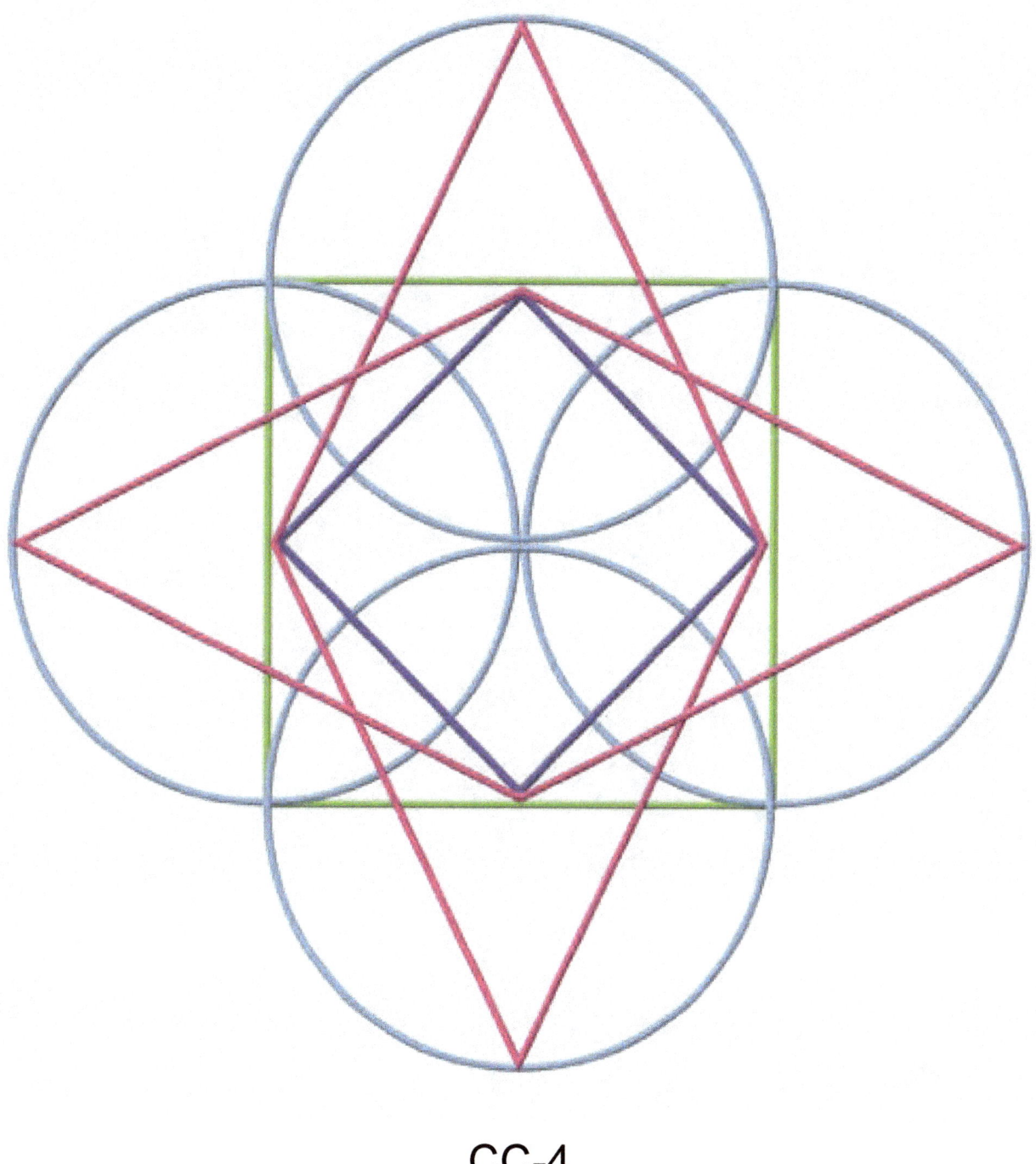

Beyond the Code

DD-1

Reprinted with Permission for noncommercial personal use only. From the Book: Beyond the Code © 2012 Donna Linn

Reprinted with Permission for noncommercial personal use only. From the Book: Beyond the Code © 2012 Donna Linn

DD-2

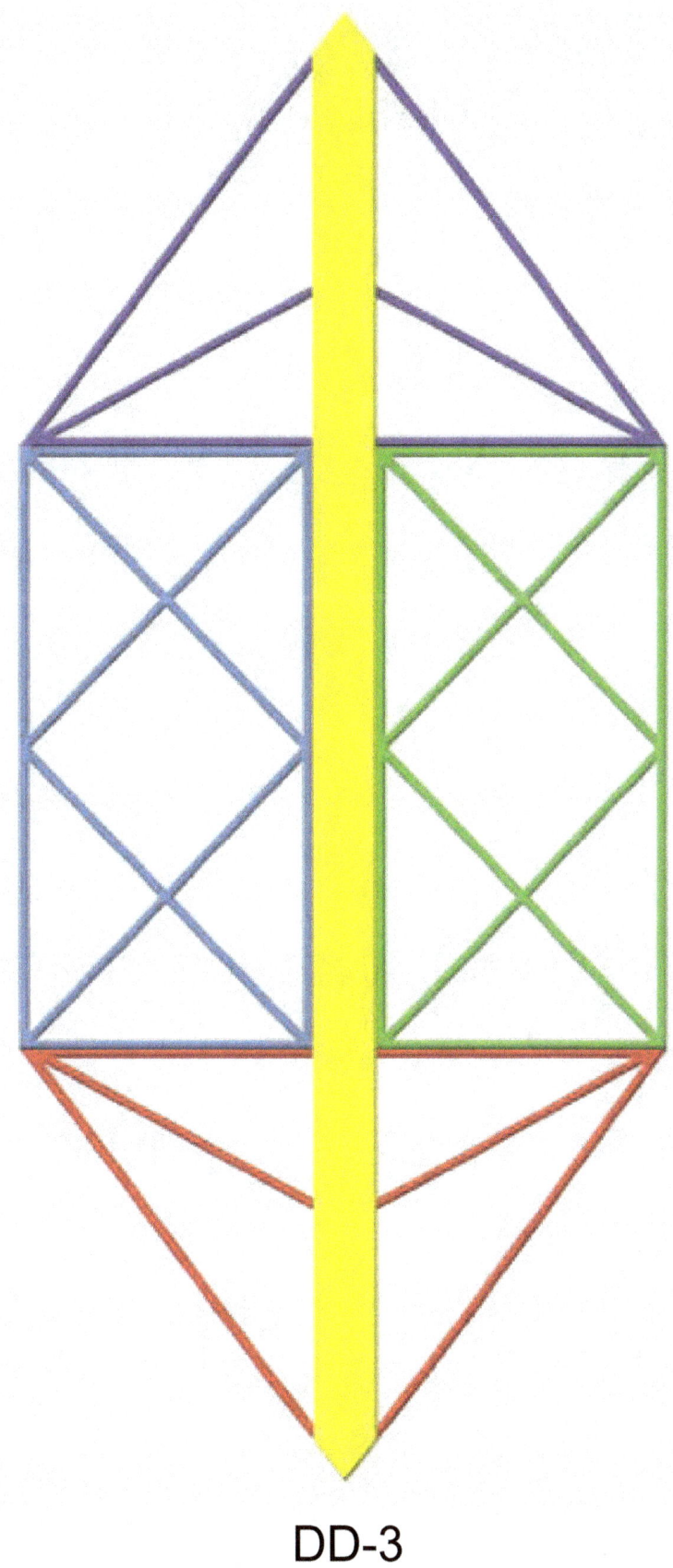

DD-3

Beyond the Code

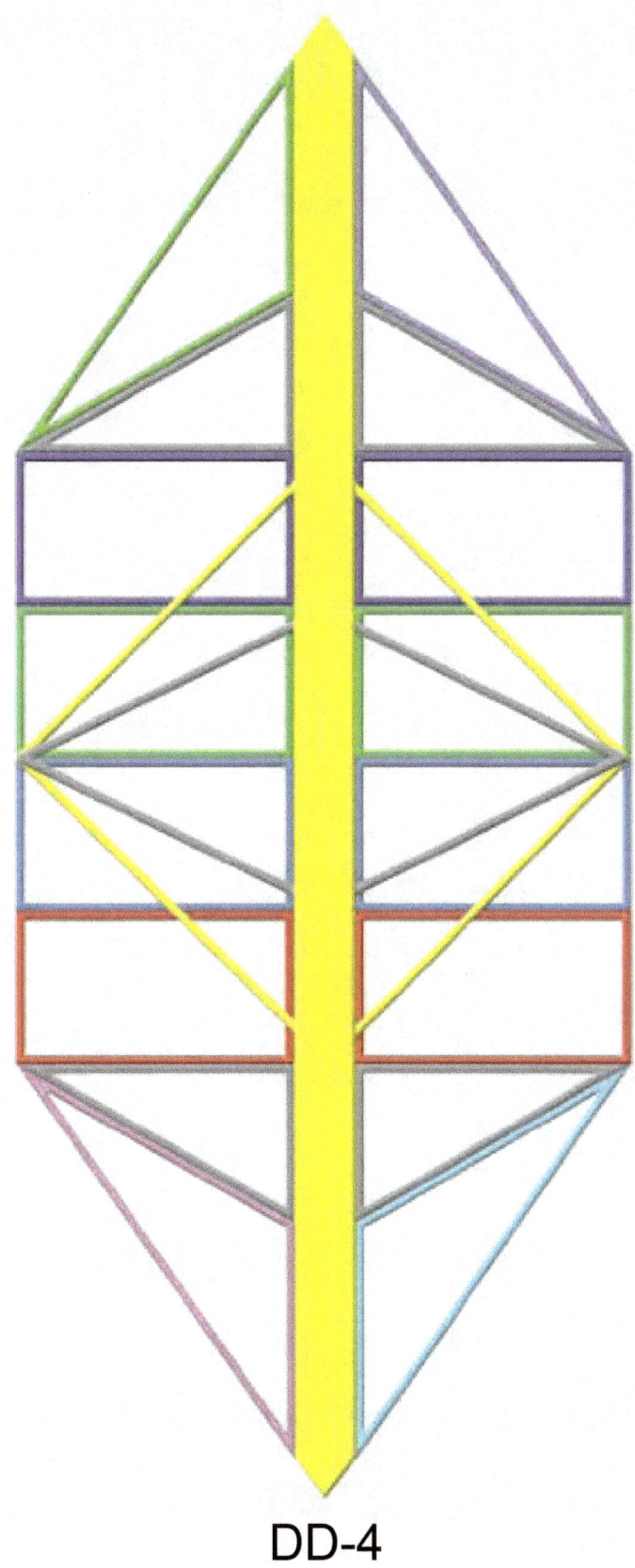

DD-4

Beyond the Code

DD-5

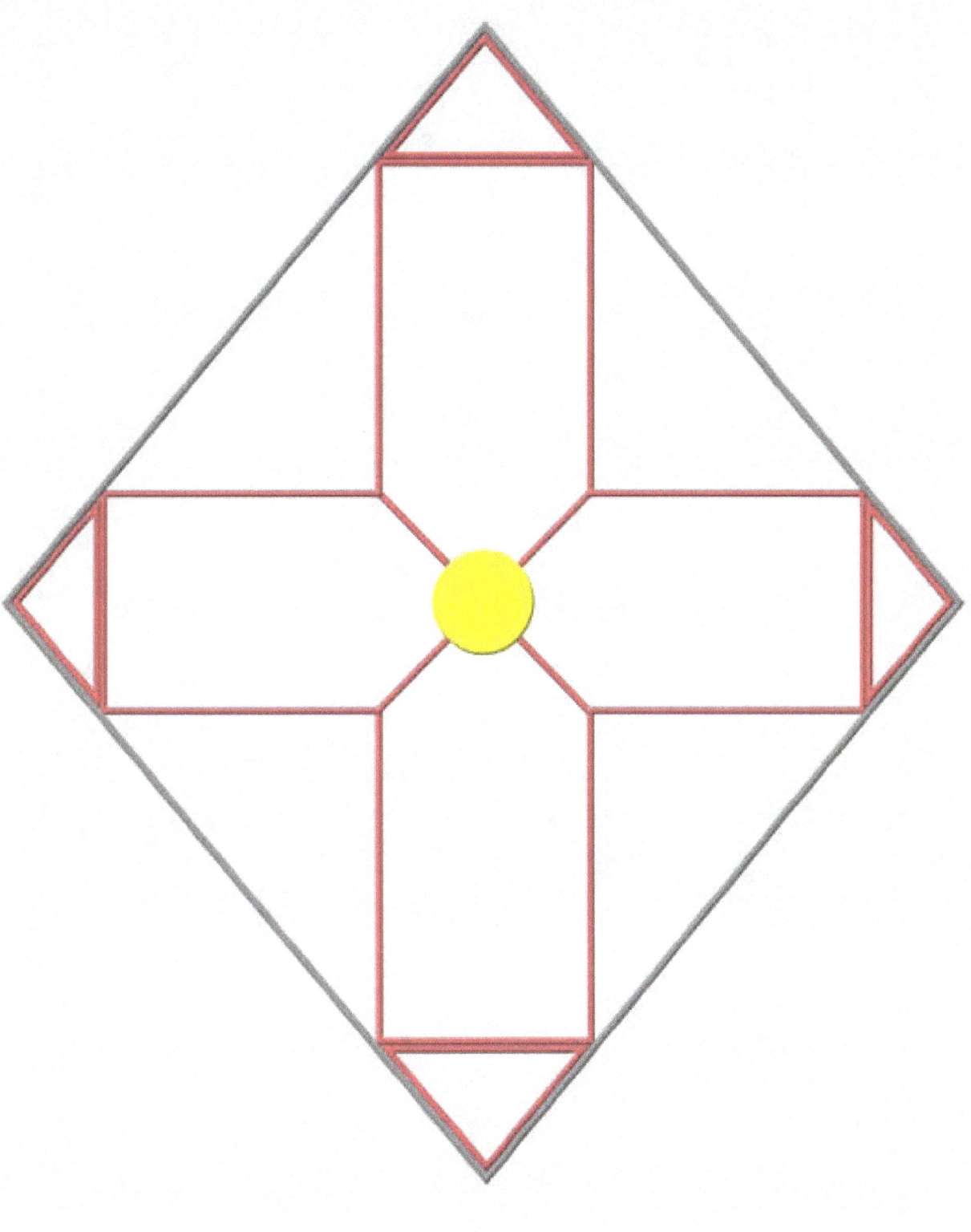

EE-1

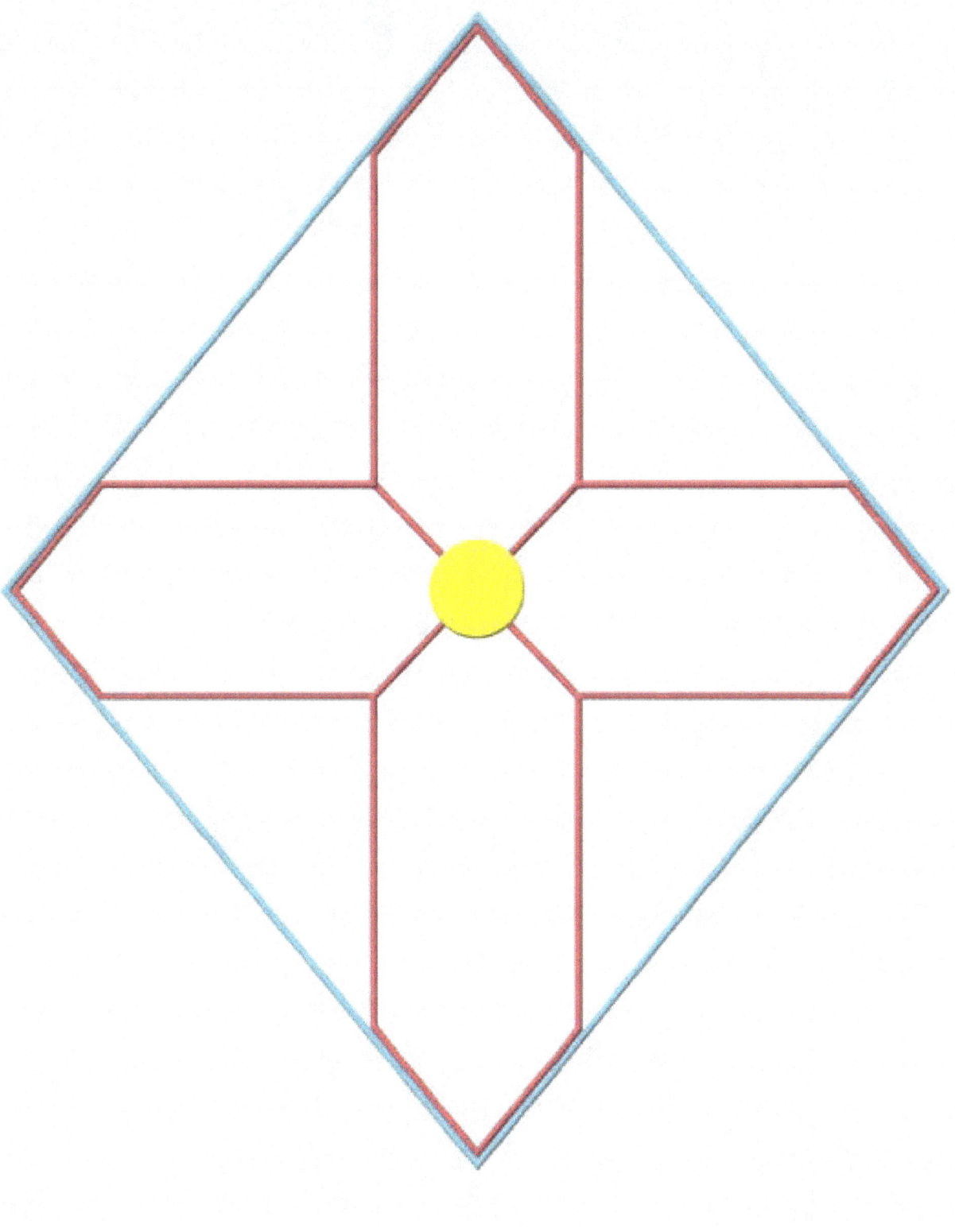

EE-2

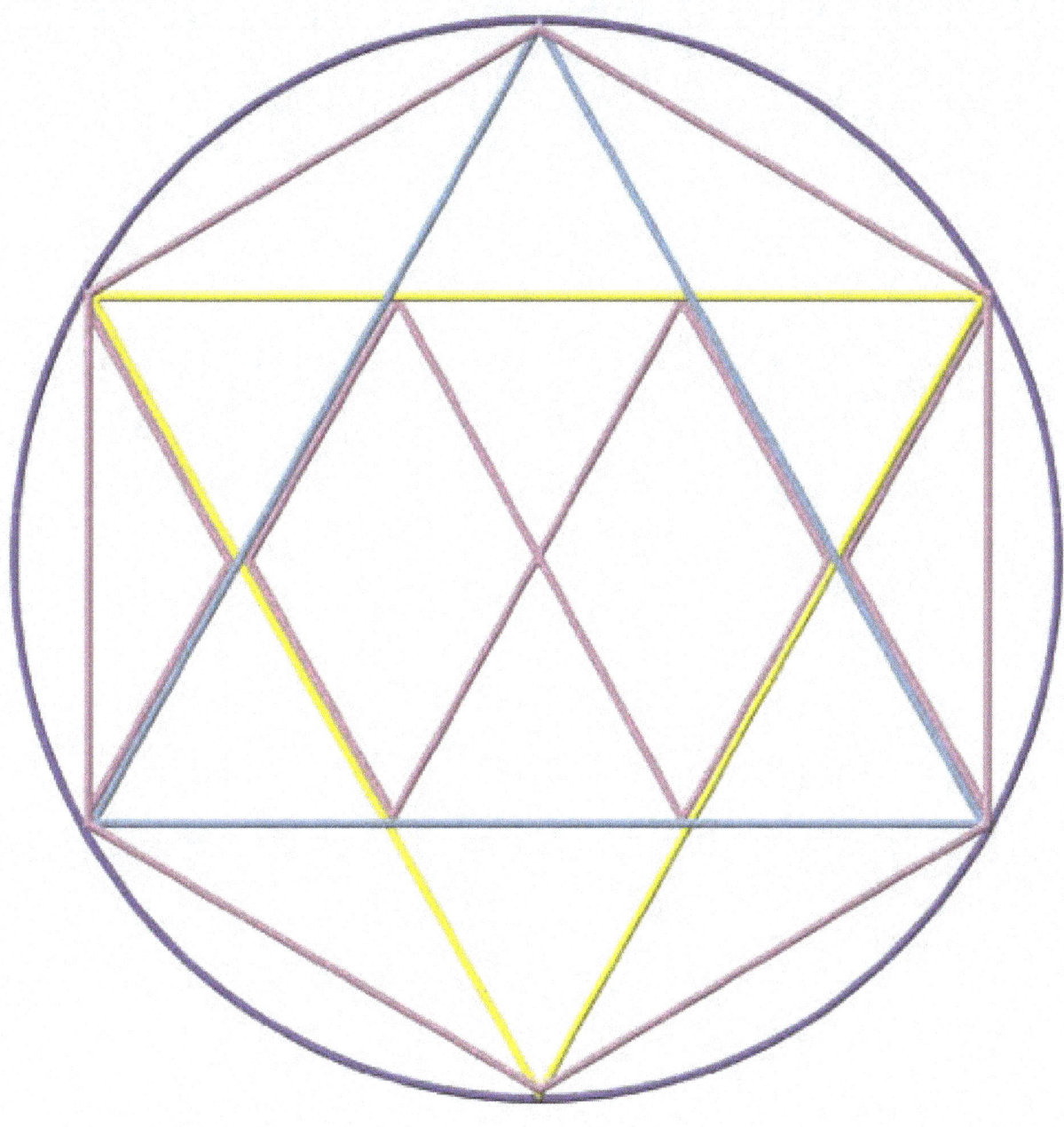

EE-3

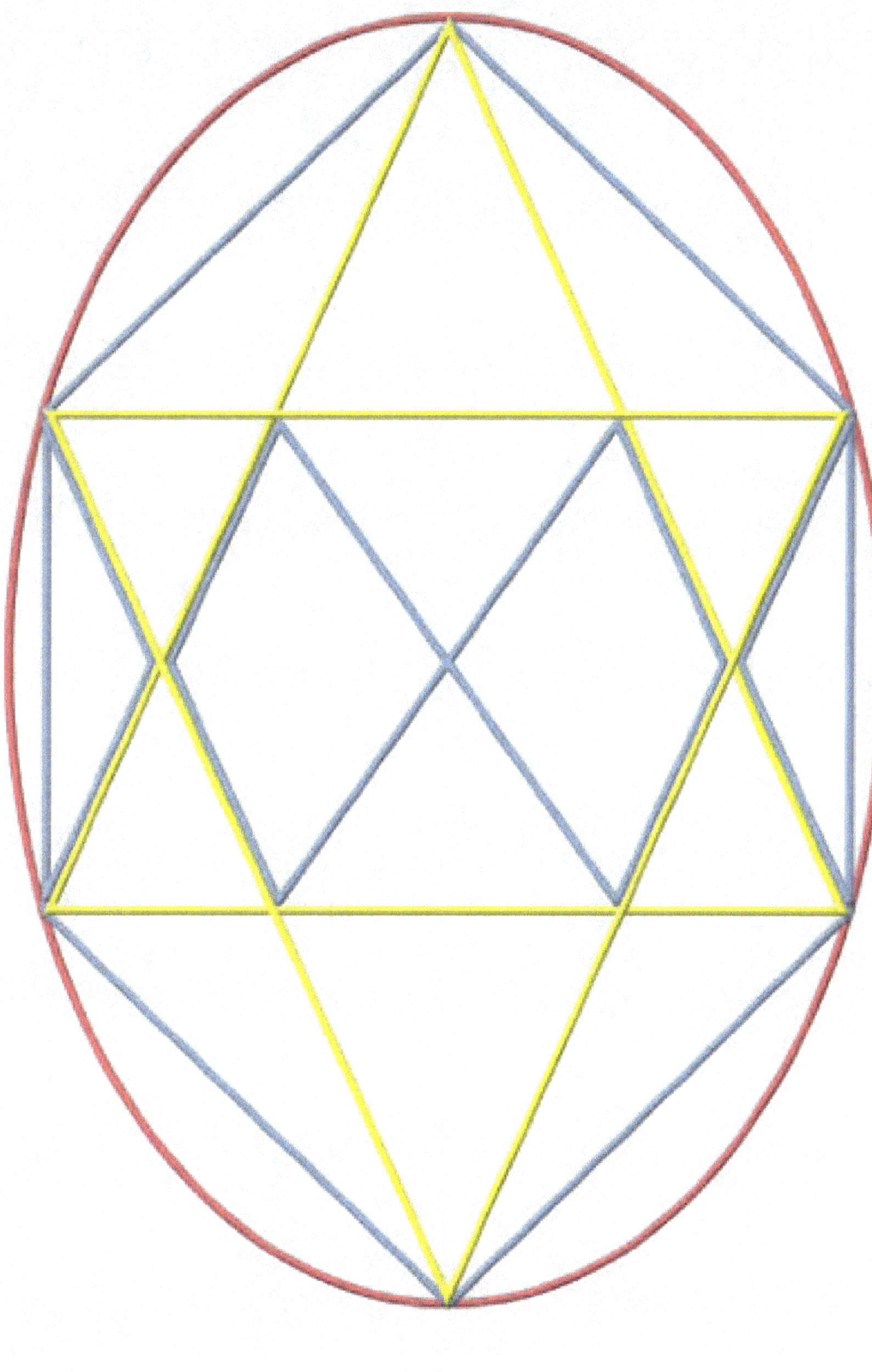

EE-4

FF-1

Beyond the Code

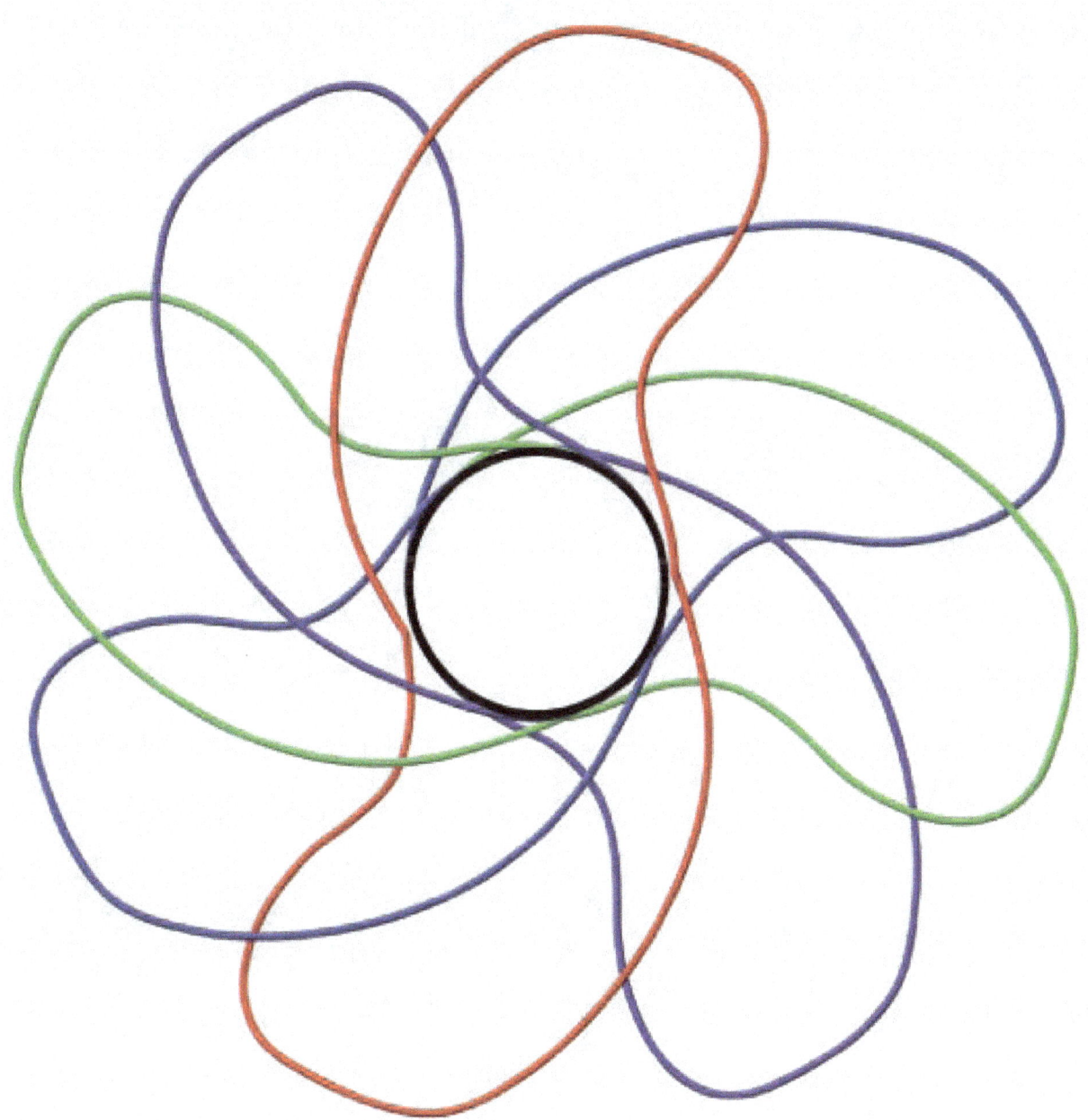

FF-2

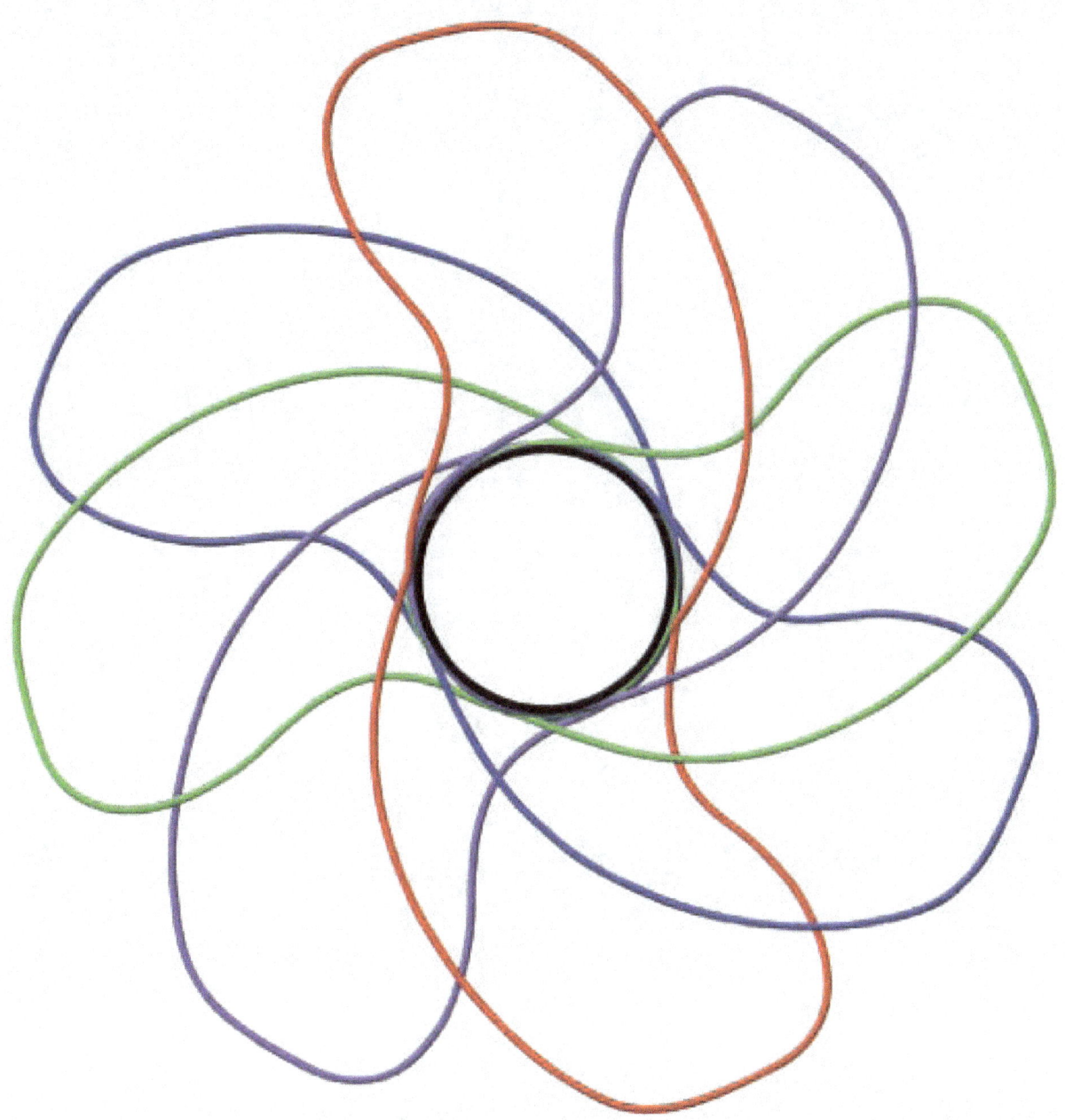

FF-3

FF-4

G-1

GG-2

Beyond the Code

HH-1

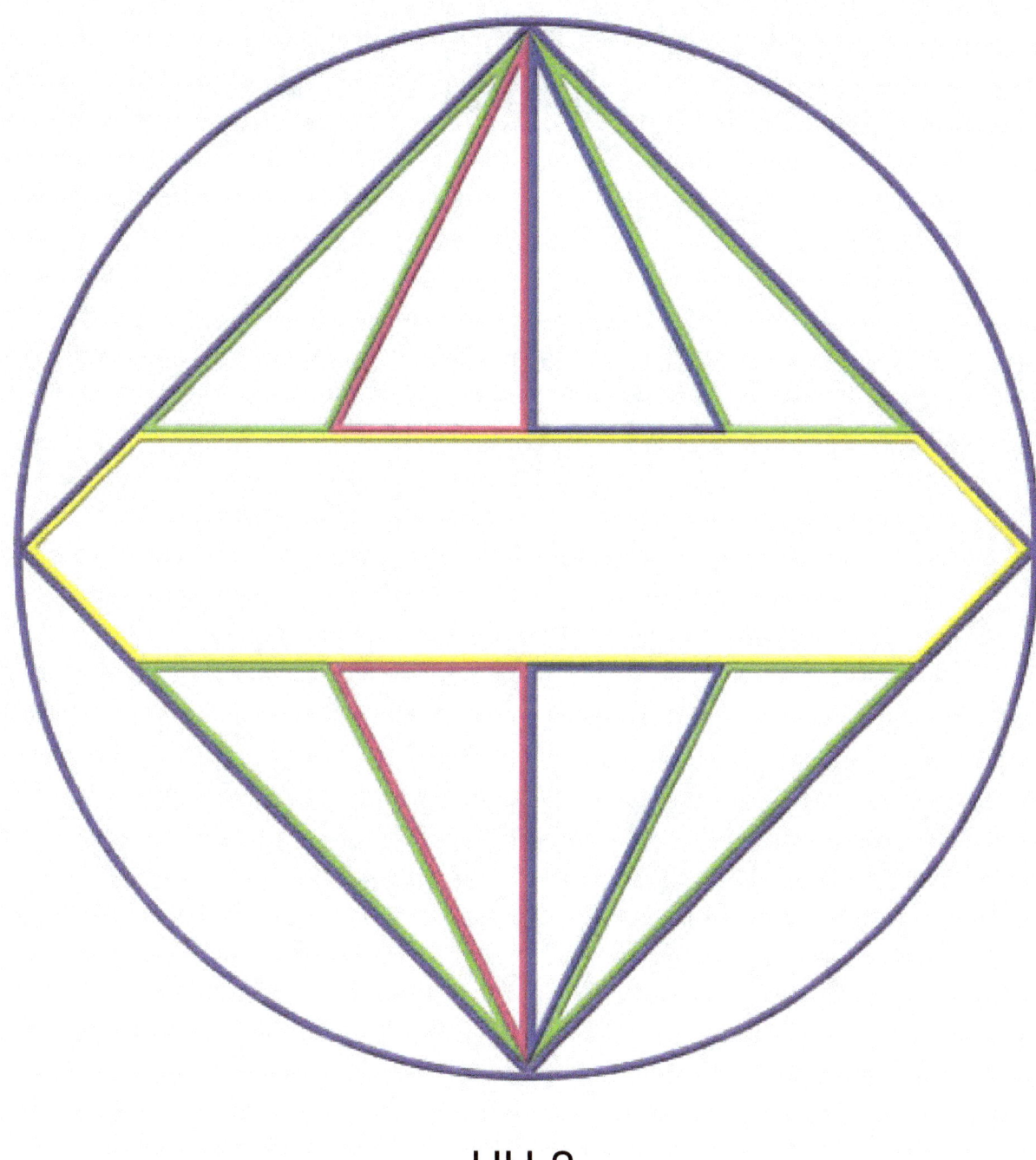

HH-2

Beyond the Code

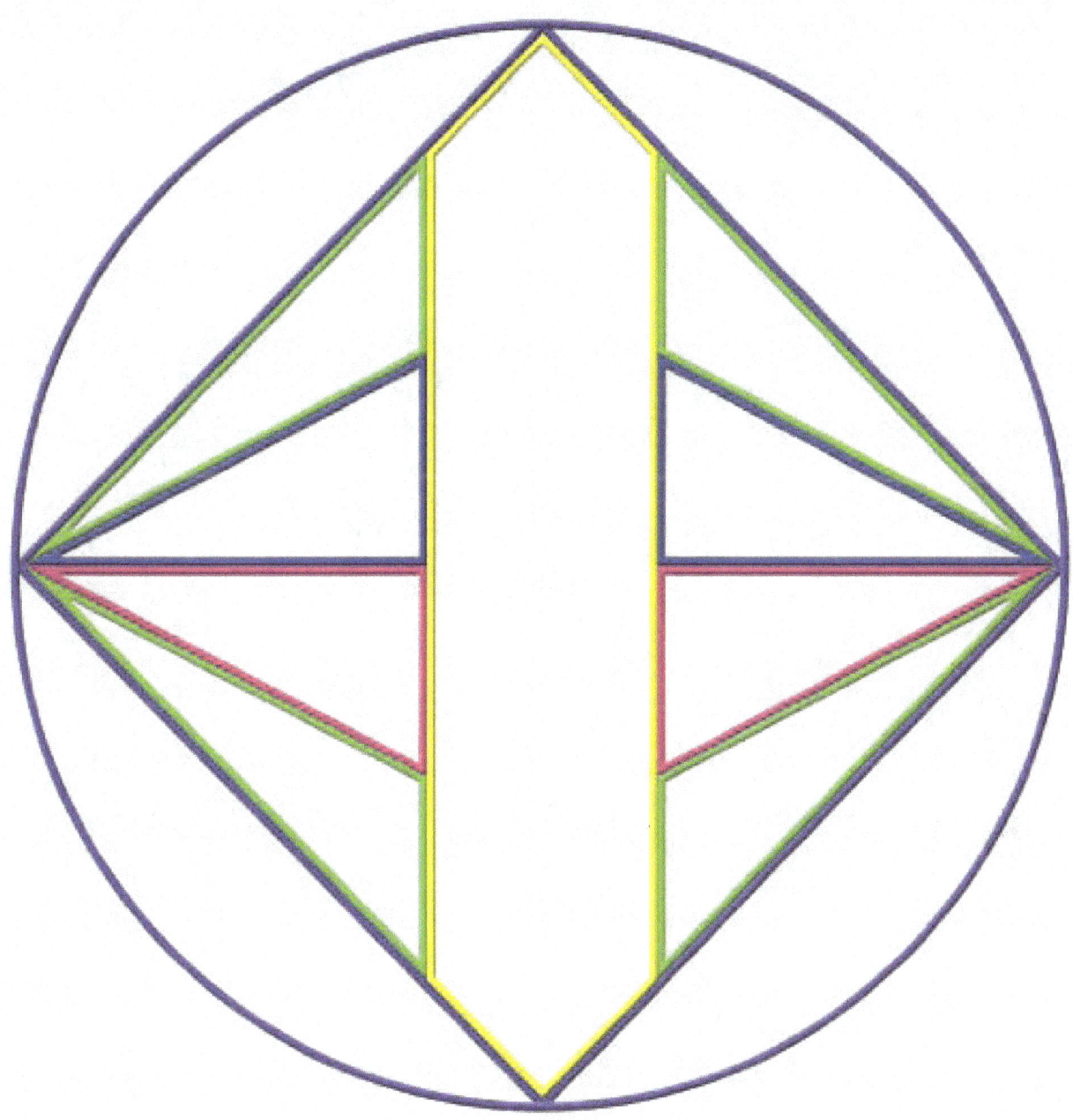

HH-3

Reprinted with Permission for noncommercial personal use only. From the Book: Beyond the Code © 2012 Donna Linn

Beyond the Code

II-1

II-2

II-3

II-4

PART THREE

PORTALS, GATEWAYS, TRANSITS, LINKS, STAND ALONES

Several of the drawings (1) did not fit with any set, or (2) worked with several sets. It was my privilege to receive information on what to call the different types.

While drawing, I became aware that there were portals and gateways, but did not really understand the differences between them. I received information on these drawings in two different channelings at different times and from different people. The first information was very simplistic and visual, because that was what I was ready to hear. The second was more in depth because I already understood how each grouping worked differently from the other. At that time, the description used was that of a **railroad station**, and the other names were given to me.

The most usual name was **PORTAL**. Generally, a portal works from inside out to a specific place. In other words, portals take you outside of yourself to another place—universe, dimension, even to Source, but they start with you. They are used when smaller amounts or pinpoint energy transfer is necessary.

GATEWAYS are for you to bring inside of yourself and learn to become something different. All you have to do is walk through the doorway provided. It is similar to a portal, except that you can open or close it from either side. It can also be thought of in terms of an end destination or a change in the current track.

LINKING pictures are just that. They link several diagrams / several sets of diagrams, similar to a train switching lever and is used to pivot the flow or destination. Links are two way. They can divert to another track and or be used to line up several of the drawings to become a very different energy.

TRANSIT drawings travel directly from terminal to terminal and are temporary. They do not add (or ramp up) energy and are used if the energy is already sufficient. They may jump past, linking to the next, or another, terminal. These pieces can take you instantly where you need or want to be. Using other drawings to add energy is sometimes needed when an energy or vibration is too low or thick for some reason.

Reprinted with Permission for noncommercial personal use only. From the Book: Beyond the Code © 2012 Donna Linn

ACCELERATORS add to the energy already available. They can be used with any of the drawings for a little more "juice", or if the energy available is not sufficient to make the "jump".

STAND-ALONES are just that. They show you what is needed and can be used singly for information or travel. Stand-alones do not need to work with any other drawings, although they can, and sometimes become portals

Again, the drawings are not labeled so that you do not have a mind-set of what you will receive. Be open, play, mix, and match. Just have fun with them and take what they give you for your experience and learning in this life.

Some of the diagrams have multiple functions and others can be programmed for specific ideas. It will be interesting to hear from others who use these, to find out more information about each one.

These are not just fun drawings, although they are that, also.

Treat them with respect.

They are sacred geometry with many different stories to tell you—and awaken you to possibilities that you may have not thought of before—or had forgotten. They are to help you learn about yourself and the higher planes, and even to give answers to question important to your life (what you need to hear, not necessarily, what you want to hear). Treat them respectfully—and be playful with them.

They are for your enjoyment, entertainment, learning, and guidance.

The codes at the bottom oof the drawings are as follows:

Portal (PRL) Gateway (GW)Linking (L)

Transit or Linking (TRL) Accelerator (AC)

Amplifier or Accelerator (AMAC)

PART FOUR

Beyond the Code

PRL-1

PRL-2

PRL-3

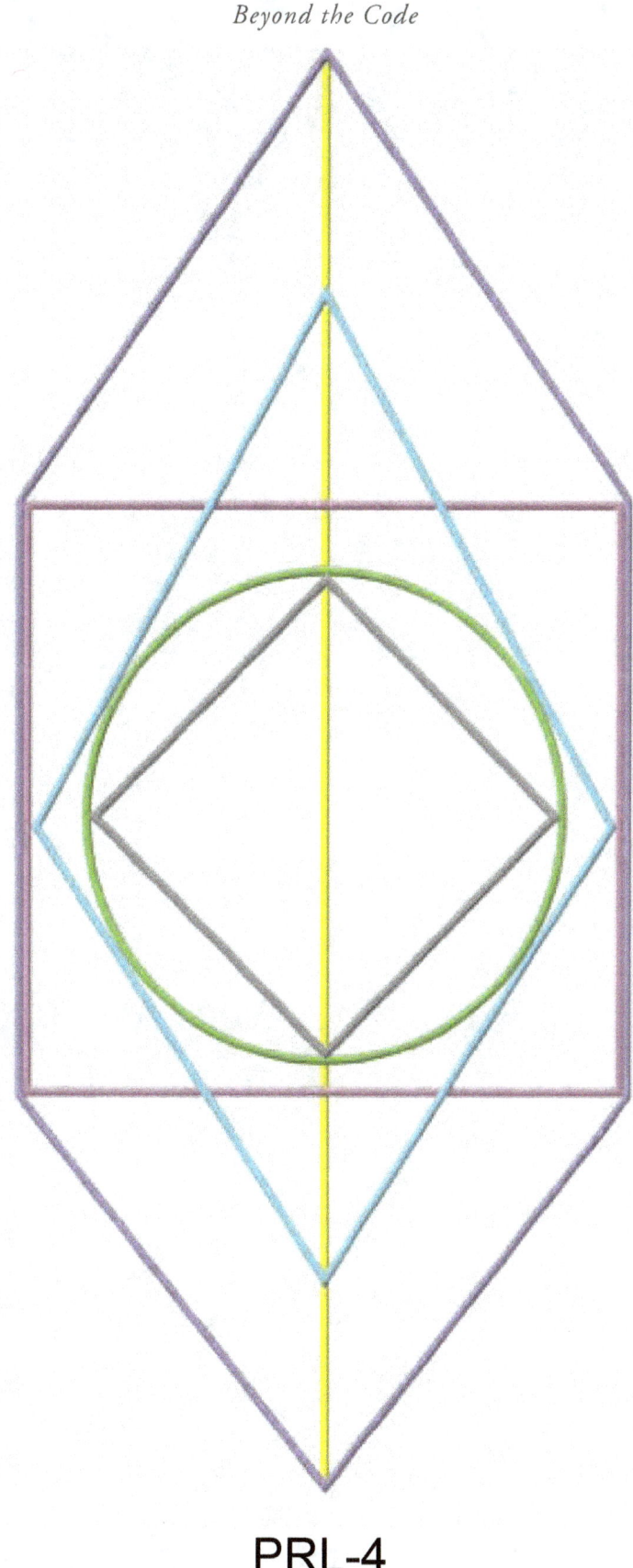

PRL-4

Beyond the Code

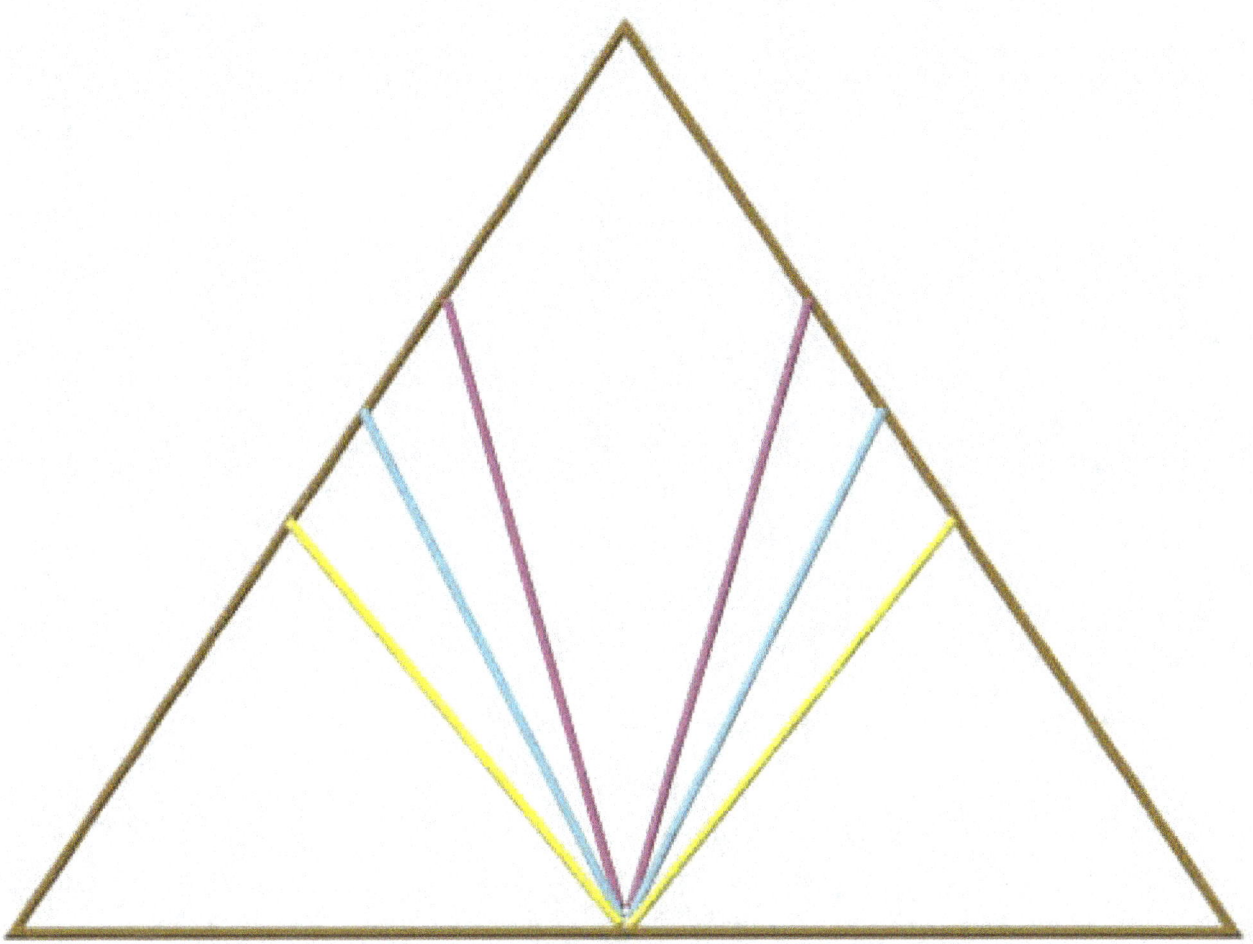

PRL-5

Beyond the Code

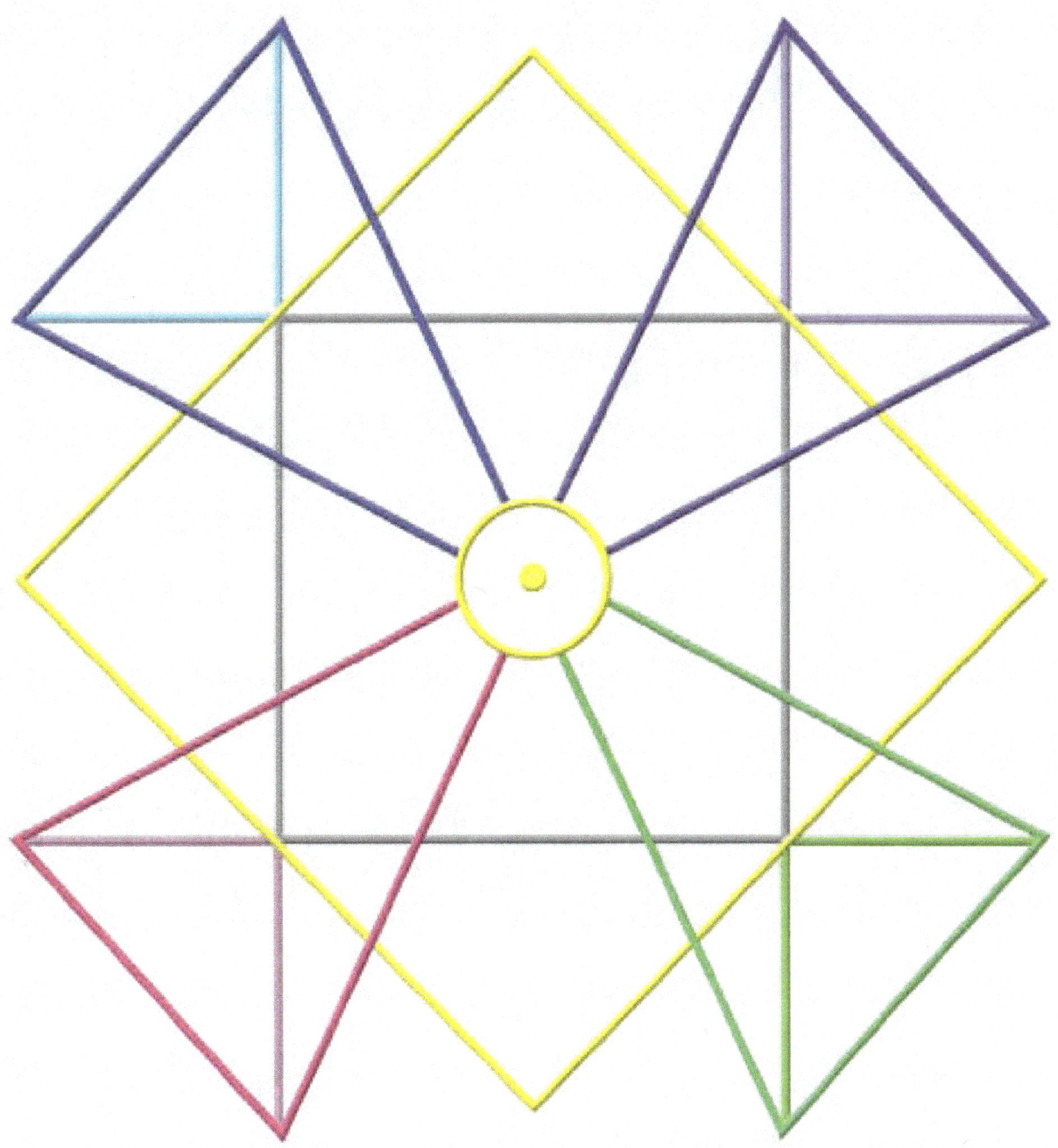

PRL-6

GW-1

Beyond the Code

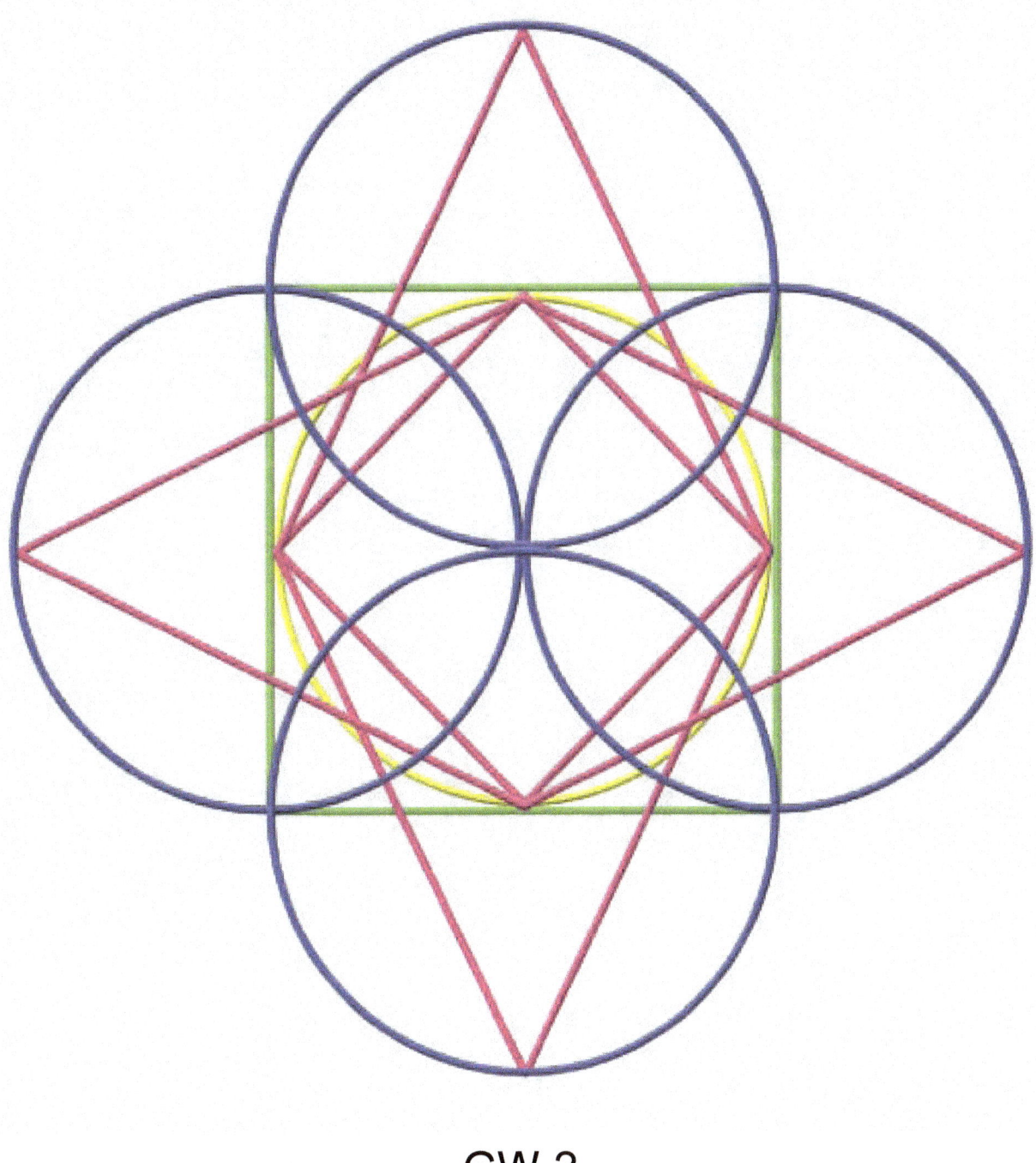

GW-2

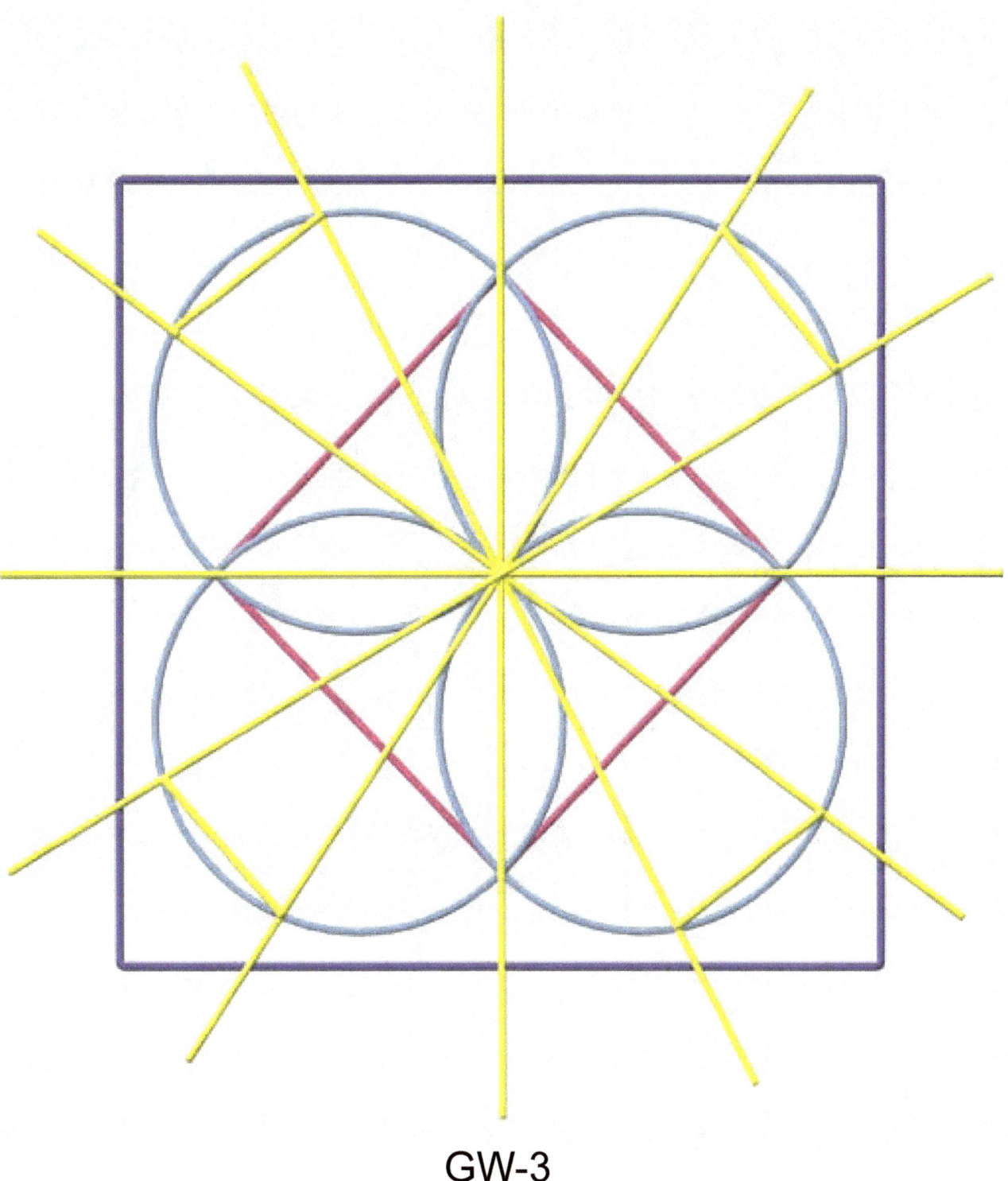

GW-3

Beyond the Code

TR-1

TR-2

Beyond the Code

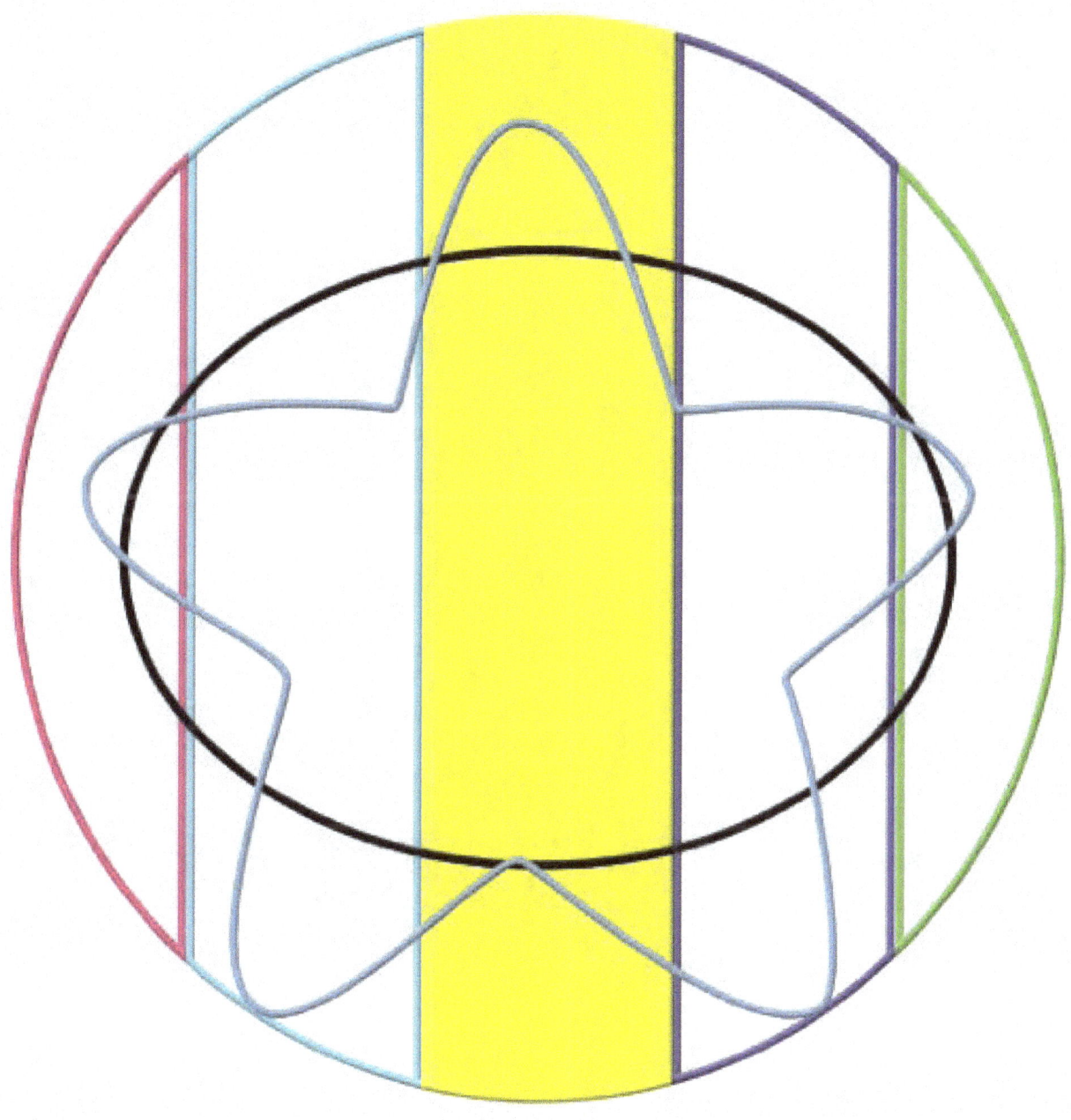

TRL-1

Beyond the Code

TRL-2

Reprinted with Permission for noncommercial personal use only. From the Book: Beyond the Code © 2012 Donna Linn

Beyond the Code

TRL-3

TRL-4

AC-1

Reprinted with Permission for noncommercial personal use only. From the Book: Beyond the Code © 2012 Donna Linn

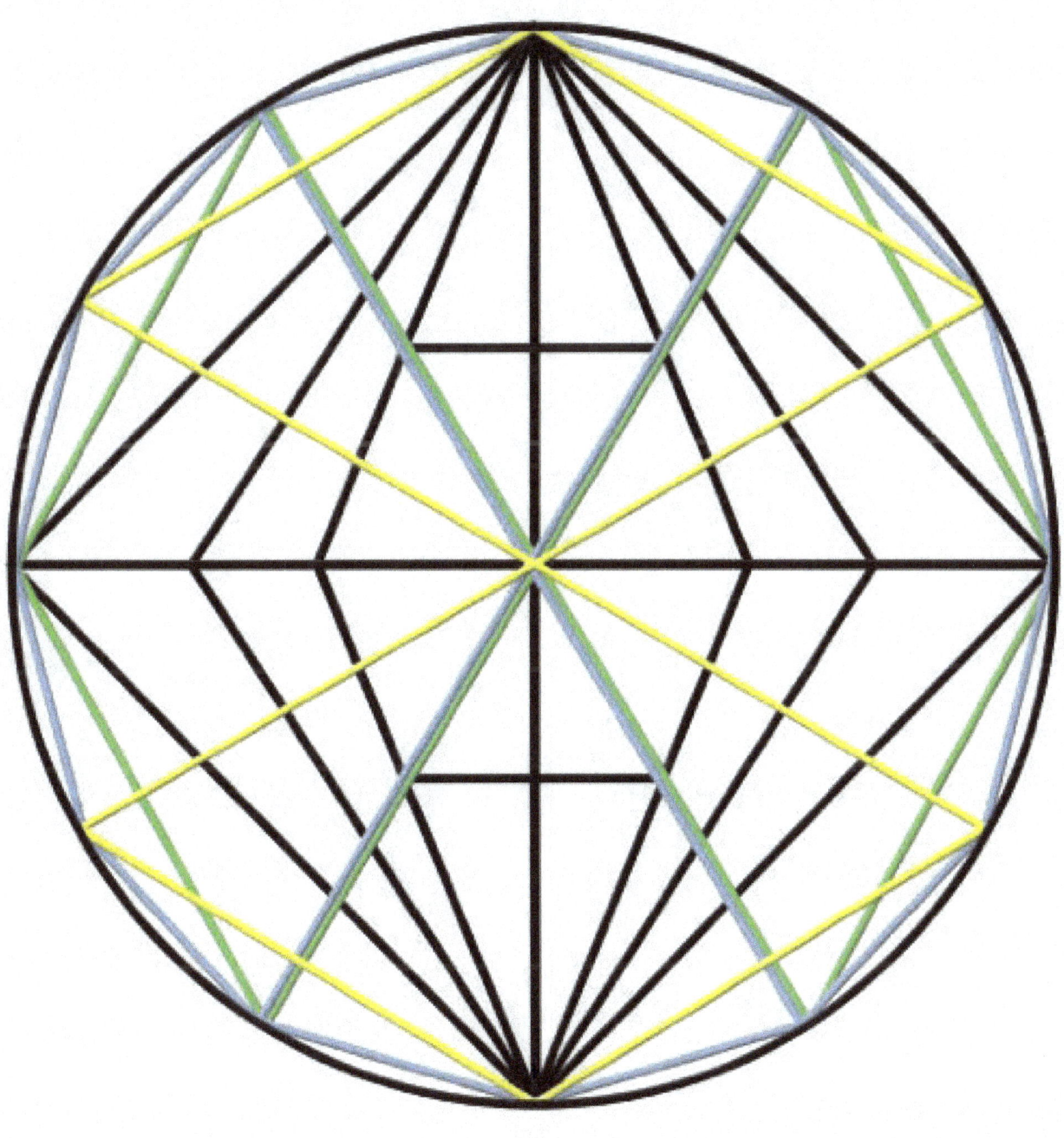

AC-2

Beyond the Code

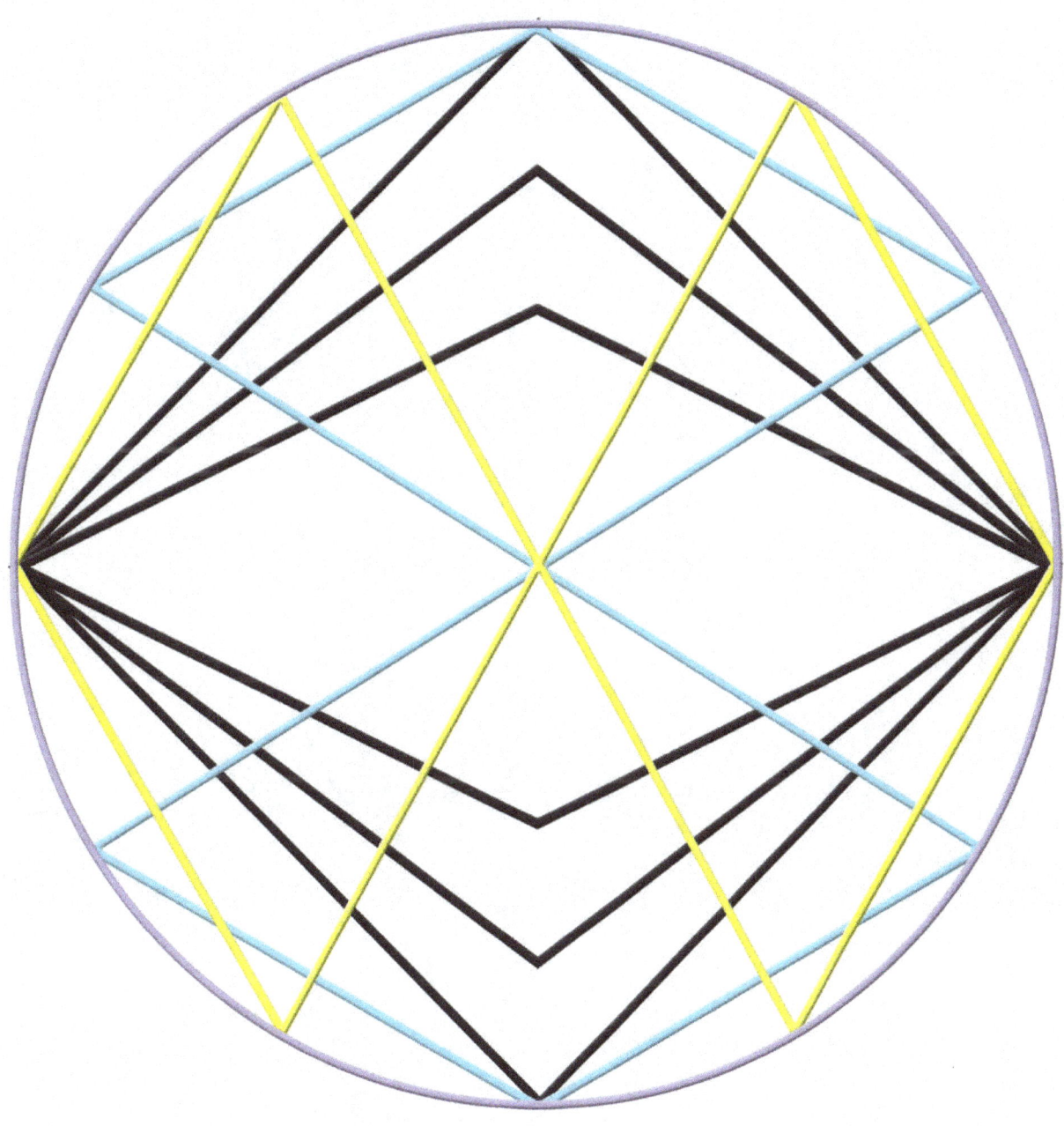

AC-3

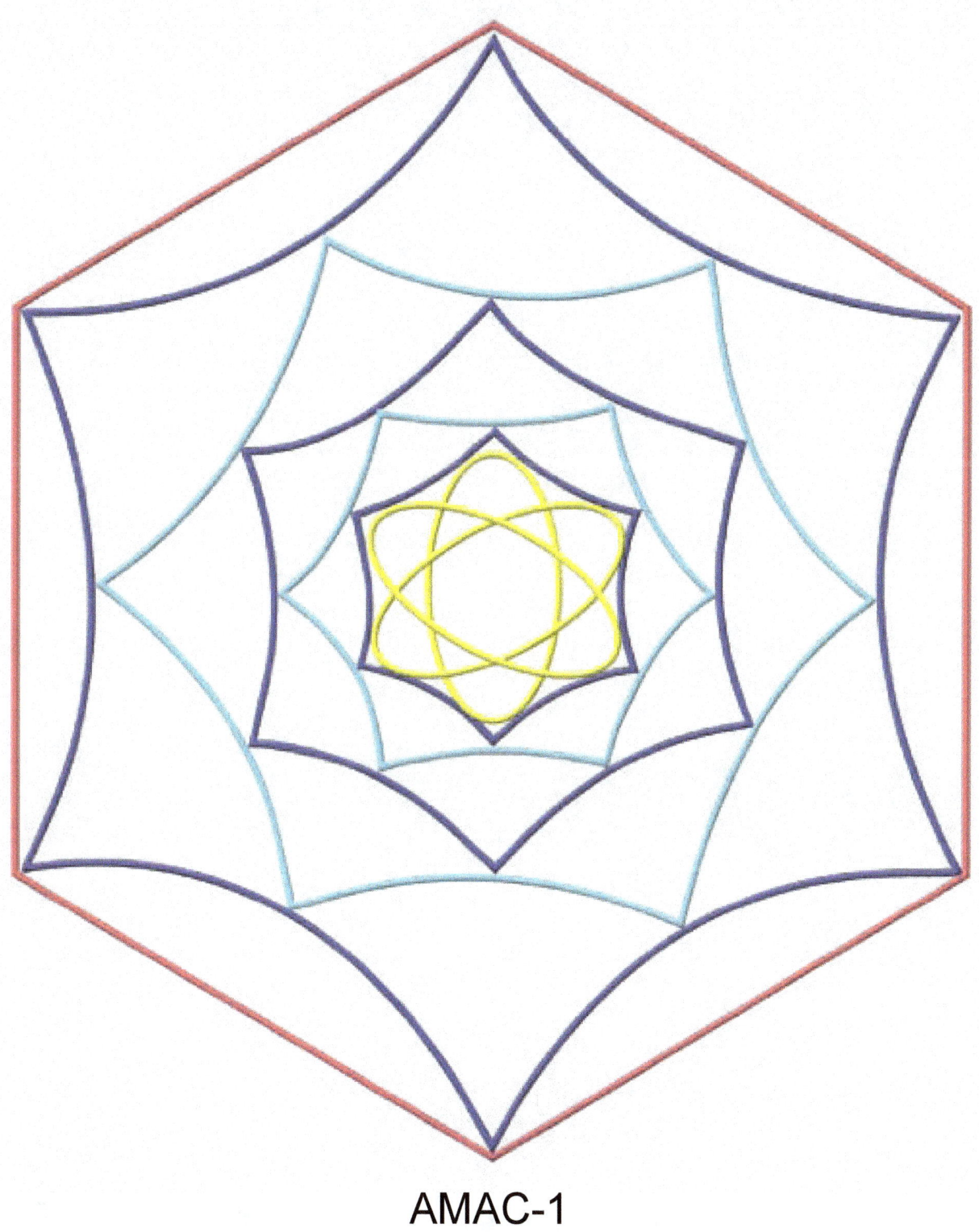

AMAC-1

AMAC-2

Beyond the Code

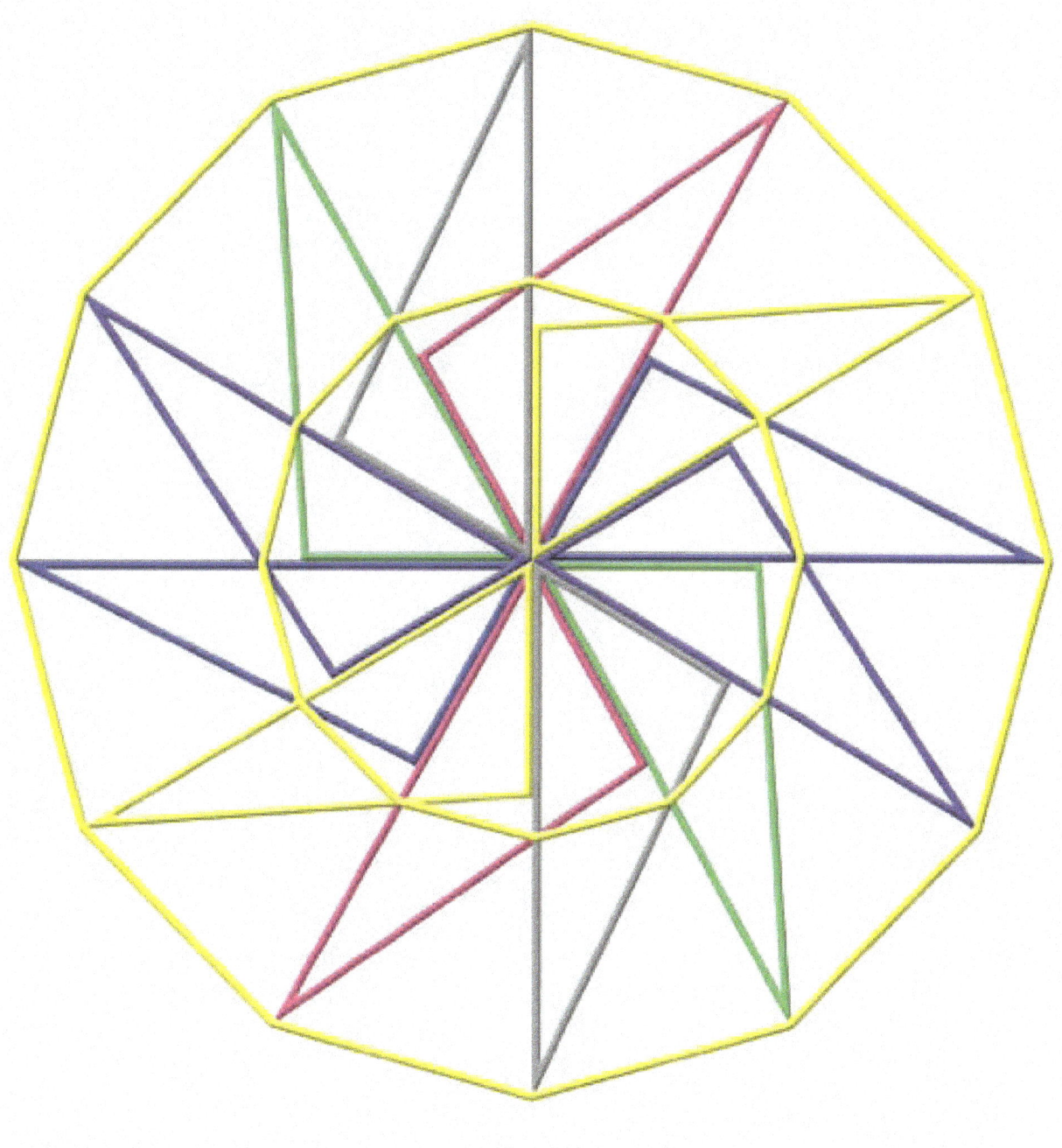

AMAC-4

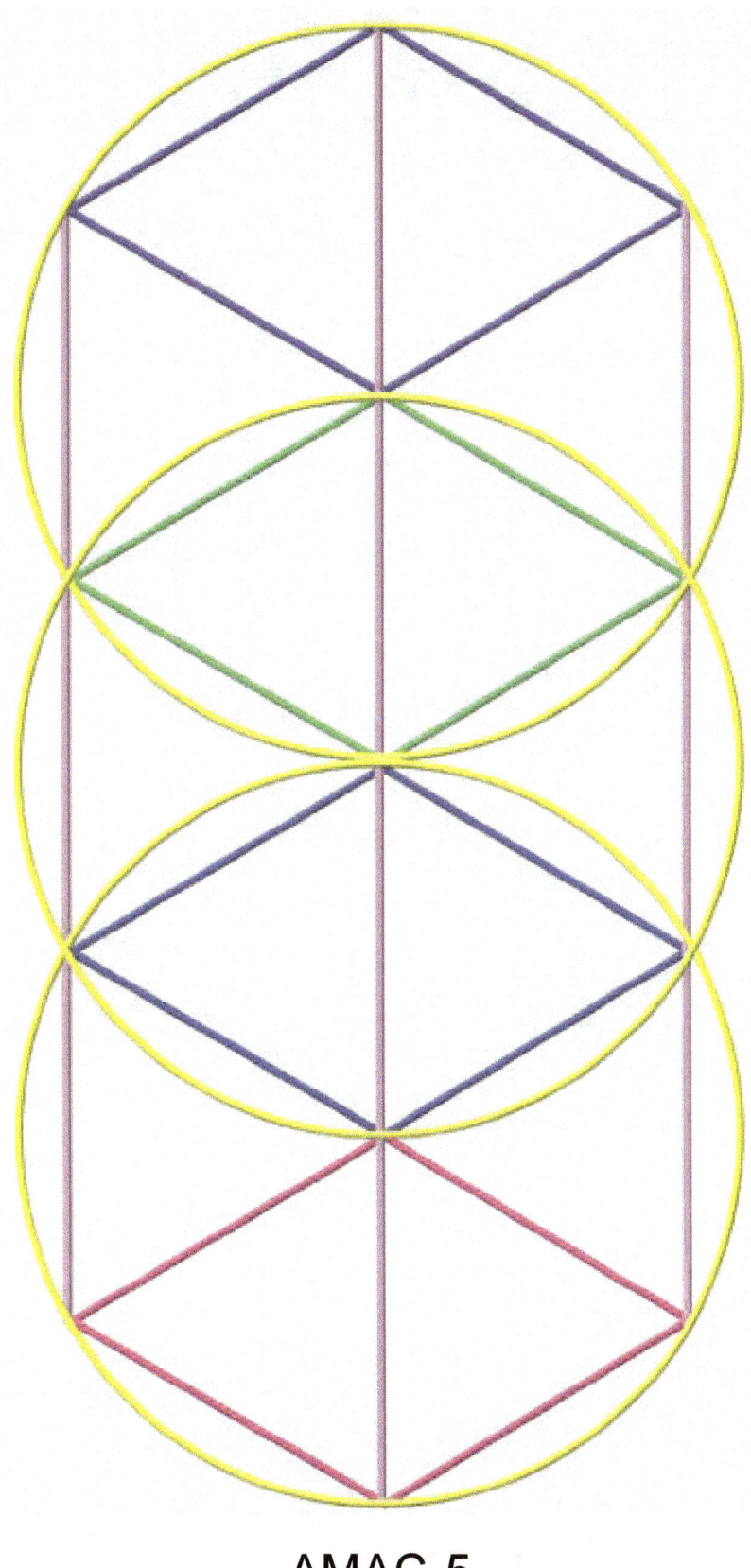

AMAC-5

Beyond the Code

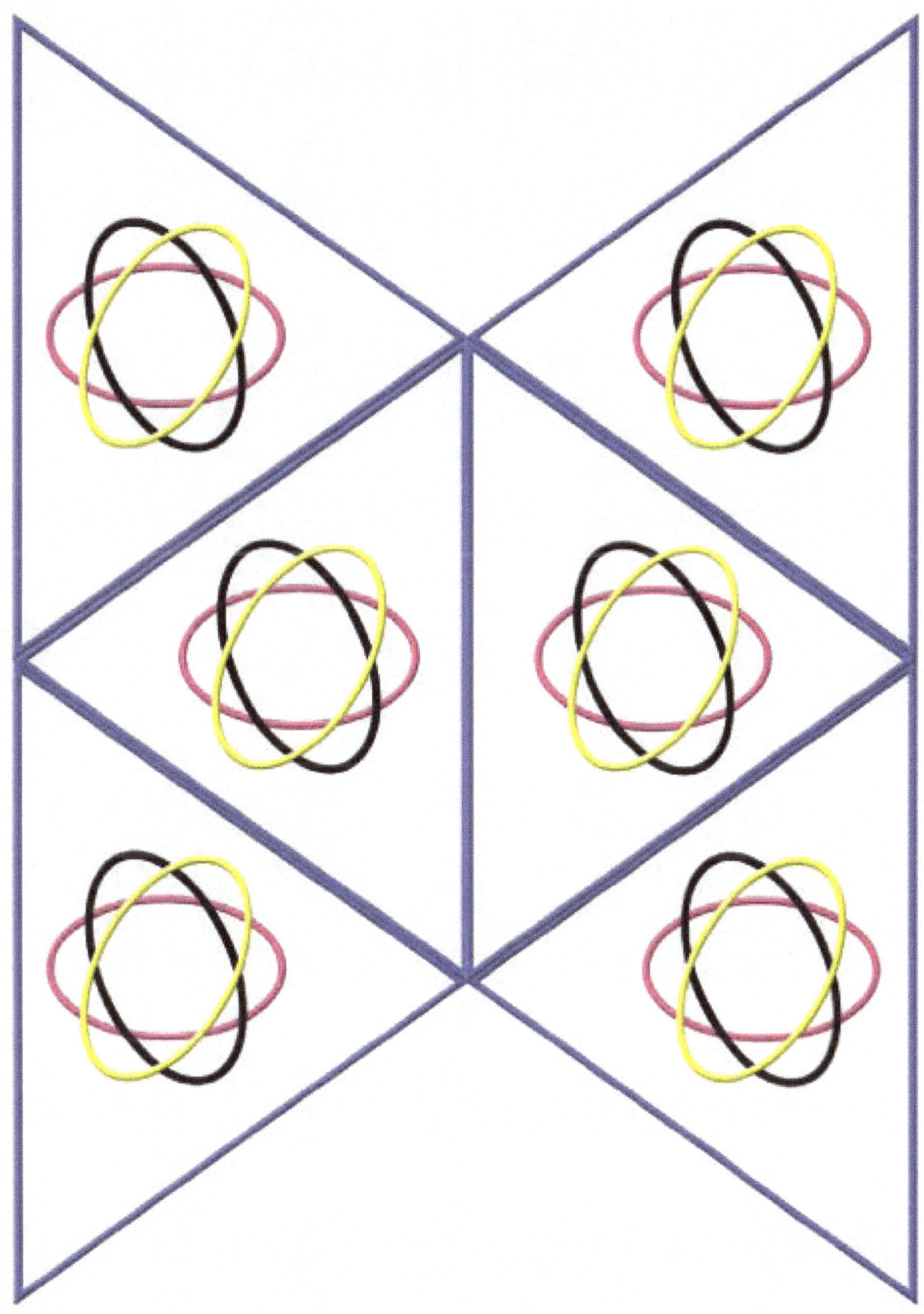

AMAC-6

Beyond the Code

ST-1

ST-2

Watching, Observing

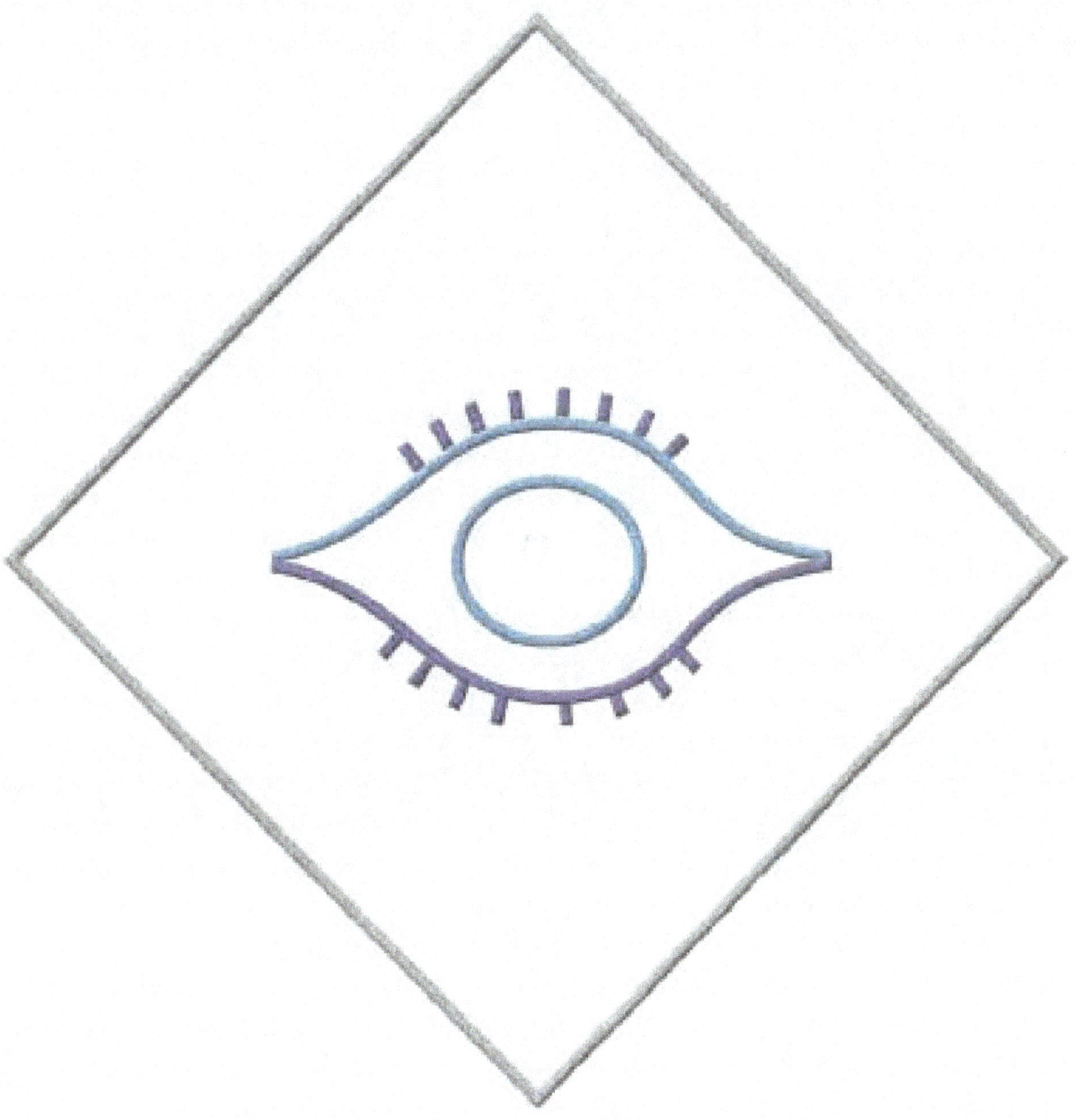

The Beginning of Everything

•

This page is intentionally left blank.

It shows possibilities and probabilities not yet conceptualized or manifested.

PART FIVE

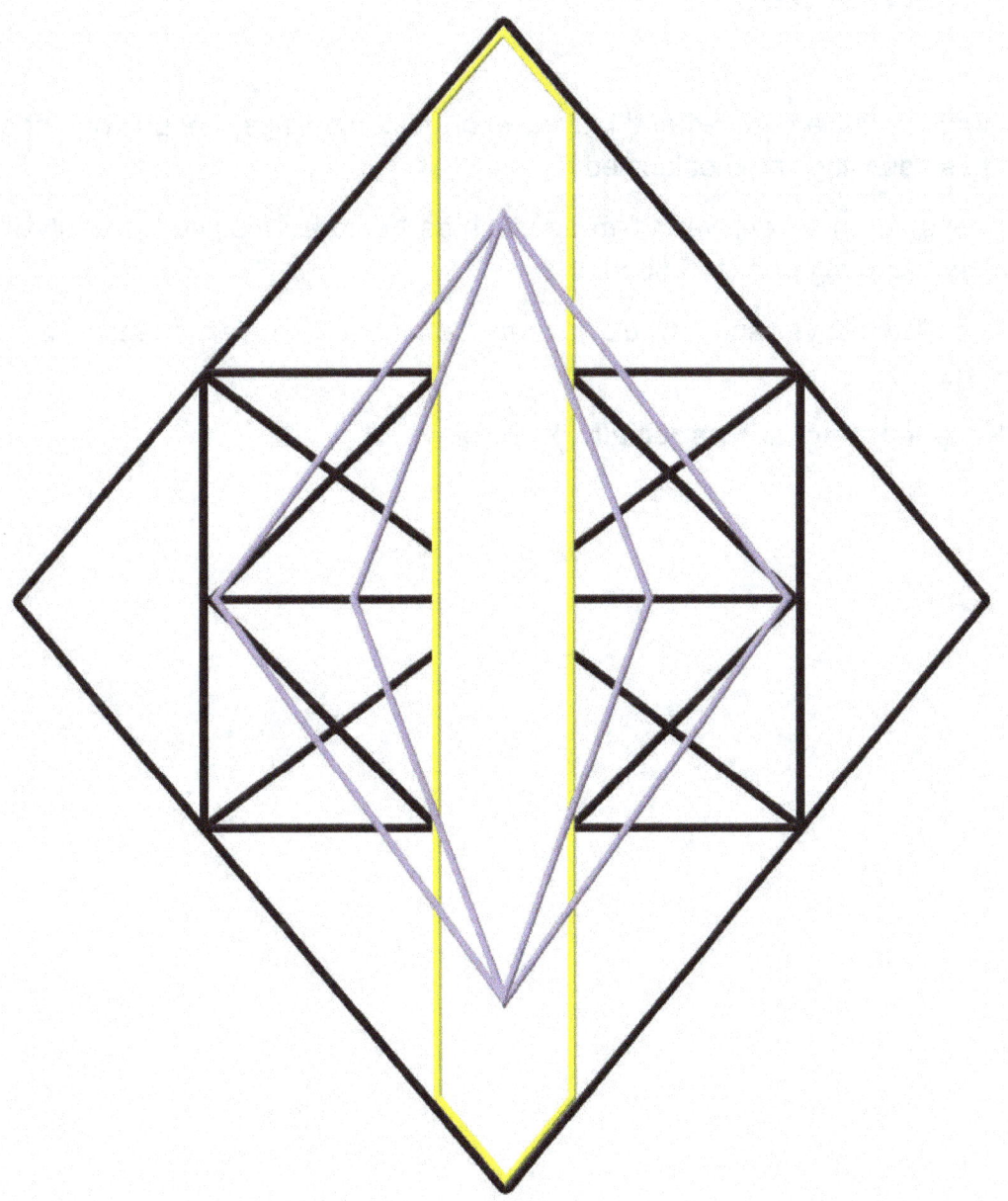

EPILOGUE

Now that you have perused and played with these drawings, I hope you understand why these drawings are not labeled.

I hope you have enjoyed them as much as I enjoyed making them, playing with them, and learning from and about them.

The "Thursdays" and I would love to hear about your experiences with these drawings.

Keep learning, and especially, keep playing!

BIBLIOGRAPHY

Adkinson, Robert, Ed. <u>Sacred Symbols: A Visual Tour of World Faith</u>. © 2009. Thames & Hudson Ltd., London, Harry Abramson New York

Ivanhoe, Omraam Mikhael. <u>The Symbolic Language of Geometrical Figures</u>. © Prosveta, 1990;   edn., Collection Izvor No. 218; translated from the French Le Langage des Figures Geometrique

Allen, Jon<u>. Drawing Geometry: A Primer of Basic Forms for Artists, Designers and Architects</u>. ©2007 Flores Books, Edinburg

Bamford, Christopher, ed. <u>Rediscovering Sacred Science</u>. Individual chapters copyrighted to individual authors. Lindisfarne Press and Floris Books 1994

Bentley, Peter J. <u>The Book of Numbers: The Secrets of Numbers and How They Created Our World</u>. © 2008. Cassell Illustrated, division of Octopus Publ. Group Limited, London

Biedermann, Hans. <u>Dictionary of Symbolism: Cultural Icons & the Meanings behind Them</u>. Tr. By James Hulbert. © 1989, tr. © 1992. Penguin Group, Meridian imprint, New York

Bruce-Mitford, Miranda. <u>The Illustrated Book of Signs and Symbols</u>. © 1996, 2004 Dorling Kindersley Ltd., London; publ. by Metro Books, New York

Cooper, J. C<u>. An Illustrated Encyclopedia of Traditional Symbols</u>. © 1978. Thames & Hudson, Ltd., London

Coxeter, H. S. M., and Greitzer, S. L. © 1967. <u>The Mathematical Associations of America</u>, Washington D. C. Regular Polygons, N.Y., Dover Publ., 1973

Critchlow, Keith. <u>Order in Space: A Design Source Book</u>. © 1969, reprinted 2000 Thames and Hudson,, Inc. New York

Elam, Kimberly. <u>Geometry of Design: Studies in Proportion and Composition</u>. © 2001 Princeton Architectural Press, New York

Reprinted with Permission for noncommercial personal use only. From the Book: Beyond the Code © 2012 Donna Linn

Farrell, Joseph, with deHart, Scott: <u>The Grid of the Gods</u>, ©2011, Adventures Unlimited Press, Kempton, Ill.

Frost, Robert. <u>Behold the Sign: Ancient Symbolism</u>. Rosicrucian Library, Vol. X. ©1940, 1972 Supreme Grand Lodge of AMORC, San Jose, Ca.

Gauding, Madonna. <u>The Signs and Symbols Bible: The Definitive Guide to Mysterious Markings</u>. © 2009, Sterling Publishing. Co. New York.

Koch, Rudolph. <u>The Book of Signs</u>. © 1955. Dover Pictorial Archive Series, Dover Publ. Inc., New York

Lawlor, Robert. <u>Sacred Geometry: Philosophy & Practice</u>. © 1982 reprinted 2007 Thames and Hudson, New York

Leff, Lawrence S. <u>Geometry: The Easy Way, third edn</u>. © 1997 Barron's Educational Series, Hauppauge, New York

Lundy, Miranda. <u>Sacred Geometry</u>. © 2001. Walker Publ. Co., New York

Lundy, Miranda. <u>Sacred Number: The Secret Qualities of Quantities</u>. ©2005 Walker Publ. Co., New York

McLeish, John. <u>Number: From Ancient Civilisations to the Computer</u> © 1991 Flamingo, an imprint of HarperCollins Publ., Hammersmiith, London

Mitchel, John, with Brown, Allan. <u>How the World Is Made</u>: The Story of Creation According to Sacred Geometry. © 2009 Inner Traditions, Rochester, Vt.

Olsen, Scott. <u>The Golden Section: Nature's Greatest Secret</u>. © 2006; Walker Publ. Co., New York

Pickover, Clifford A.: <u>From Pythagoras to the 57th Dimension</u>, 250 Milestones in the History of Mathematics © 2009. Sterling Publ. Co., New York

Quadrivium: <u>The Four Classical Liberal Arts of Number, Geometry, Music, and Cosmology</u>, separate books with their own copyright as one book © 2010 Walker Publ. Co., New York

Schimmel, Annemarie. <u>The Mystery of Numbers</u>. © 1993. Oxford University Press, New York, Oxford

Schneider, Michael S. <u>A Beginner's Guide to Constructing the Universe</u>: The Mathematical Archetypes of Nature, Art, and Science; A voyage from 1-10. © 1994. HarperCollins Publ., New York

Shesso, Renna. <u>Math for Mystics</u>. © 2007. Red Wheel/Weiser, San Francisco, Ca.

Reprinted with Permission for noncommercial personal use only. From the Book: Beyond the Code © 2012 Donna Linn

Skinner, Stephen. <u>Sacred Geometry: Deciphering the Code</u>. © 2006 by Octopus Publishing Group, Ltd., London. 2006 Sterling Publishing Co., New York.

Stewart, Malcolm. <u>Patterns of Eternity: Sacred Geometry and the Starcut Diagram</u>. © 2009 Floris Books, Edinburgh

Sutton, Andrew. <u>Ruler & Compass: Practical Geometric Constructions</u>. © 2009 Walker Publ. Co., New York

Sutton, Daud. <u>Platonic and Archimedean Solids: The Geometry of Space</u>. © 2002; Walker Publ. Co., New York

About the Author

DONNA LINN and her husband owned a metaphysical center/store in Ft. Thomas, Kentucky for 11 years (1990-2001).

They sold crystals, jewelry, books, herbs, had many classes, guest lectures, but concentrated on energy healing (Reiki at that time the most usual). There were times when three or four tables of Reiki ran simultaneously at the store during a weekly evening gathering after the store closed. Meditation, self-development, and psychic classes were also taught by them or guests. They also sold herbs and Donna gave lectures on the historical value of herbs around the area.

Even before that time they were very active within the metaphysical communities in Cincinnati, Ohio and Northern Kentucky. They also wholesaled crystals to the other metaphysical stores.

Donna also teaches a two-part workshop on esoteric numerology, using the numbers 1-26 (instead of 1-9) for a name reading, with additional numbers to chart and understand. The second part teaches how to use birthdates to find important years within specific areas (physical, mental, emotional and spiritual).

Teaching Galactic Healing, a relatively new and very powerful energy healing method since 2007 is also available. It combines three levels of symbols for healing on the physical, emotional, mental and spiritual levels as necessary for the individual's highest good.

Donna Linn is available for lectures/workshops on this information. Please contact her by email 2donnamessic@gmail.com.

Reprinted with Permission for noncommercial personal use only. From the Book: Beyond the Code © 2012 Donna Linn

Other books written by the author:

Breaking the Code: Numerology with a twist

Beyond the Code: Energy with Sacred Geometry

Inside the Code: Numerology within the I Ching

Decoding Universal Energy and Healing
- The 4 I's - Healing Methods - Resources

Using the Code: A Continuation of Beyond the Code Numerology

Reprinted with Permission for noncommercial personal use only. From the Book: Beyond the Code © 2012 Donna Linn

www.ingramcontent.com/pod-product-compliance
Lightning Source LLC
Chambersburg PA
CBHW082150070526
44585CB00020B/2153